SONG OF THE GHOST IN THE MACHINE

SONG OF THE GHOST IN THE MACHINE

Roger Horrocks

VICTORIA UNIVERSITY PRESS

VICTORIA UNIVERSITY PRESS
Victoria University of Wellington
PO Box 600 Wellington
http://vup.victoria.ac.nz

National Library of New Zealand Cataloguing-in-Publication Data

Horrocks, Roger.
Song of the ghost in the machine / Roger Horrocks.
ISBN 978-0-86473-985-8
I. Title.
NZ821.3—dc 23

Printed by PrintStop, Wellington

CONTENTS

CONTENTS

1. WALKING

He who sees, senses that he is seeing; he who hears, senses that he is hearing; he who walks, senses that he is walking, and thus for all the other activities there is something that senses that we are exerting them, in such a way that if we sense, we sense that we are sensing, and if we think, we sense that we are thinking. This is the same thing as sensing existence . . . [and] sensing that we are alive is in and of itself sweet . . .
—Aristotle

Never did I exist so completely, never live so thoroughly, never was so much myself, if I dare use the expression, as in those journeys made on foot. Walking animates and enlivens my spirits . . . [it can] conspire to free my soul, and give boldness to my thoughts, throwing me, in a manner, into the immensity of beings, where I combine, choose and appropriate them to my fancy, without constraint or fear.
—Jean-Jacques Rousseau

From the sublime to the ridiculous is but a step.
—Attributed to Napoleon Bonaparte, as recorded by Abbé du Pradt

I am alarmed when it happens that I have walked a mile into the woods bodily, without getting there in spirit. In my afternoon walk I would fain forget all my morning occupations, and my obligations to society. But it sometimes happens that I cannot easily shake off the village. The thought of some work will run in my head, and I am not where my body is – I am out of my senses. . . . What business have I in the woods, if I am thinking of something out of the woods?
—Henry David Thoreau

The primary motor cortex, basal ganglia, and cerebellum, which coordinate physical movement, also coordinate the movement of thought.

7

Just as they order the physical movements needed for moving, they order the sequence of thoughts needed for thinking.
—John J. Ratey

According to Lakoff and Johnson, time is universally viewed as a journey in which we see someone – ourselves perhaps – walking along a footpath towards the future and away from the past.
—Bernard J. Baars

Walk past these houses on a Sunday morning
with a piano stumbling in the front room. . . .
Somewhere there is value to them. As the piano stumbles
something grows into being. It will take shape in the end.
—Kendrick Smithyman, 'Walk Past These Houses on a Sunday Morning'

Solvitur ambulando. [You can solve it by walking.]
—Lewis Carroll, 'What the Tortoise Said to Achilles'

FIRST WALK

Begin with one of the simplest things, walking.
Another morning, another breathing space.
New clouds in the sky in the land of the living,
and I head out into this sample corner of the earth,
blinking at its intricacy in the cool morning light.
My feet and shadow drift. I wonder what
to make of them and where to take them
in a streetscape as 'beautiful as the chance encounter
of an umbrella and a sewing machine on a dissecting table.'

After more than twenty thousand days in this world
I'm back to basics. My body is dated equipment
and I ride it as though I've borrowed it
for the day, taking its senses on a test flight.

Walking works best if you don't think how,
when it's par for the course, like breathing. Right
brain left foot, left brain
right foot, four feet a second,
but cease to count or you'll lose the knack.
The absolute logic of forwards: pendulum dynamics,
lifting yourself by your own bootstraps.

No man steps twice into the same
one-way street. This mind that still has unused
storage space, this generic human being
in well-worn shoes is a secret agent assigned
to case this ordinary street. 'Let us possess
one world: each has one
and is one.' Objects stare back.

A cluster of branches quivers in the wind, a gate
swings and bangs. Drops gleam on a leaf
as though waiting for my eyes. Fingers tingle
as I touch the sun-warmed metal of a fence.
I clasp things in the palms of thought – birds'
shrill cries, the smell of mown grass –
and taste their presence. Are the day's details
more tangible, more real than our frail ideas?

Sometimes the subject, often the object, always
the verb, we struggle to grasp the whole untidy
grammar of our existence, a sentence as long as the world.

SECOND WALK

Step out this morning into winter space,
textured by fog, wind, pinpricks of rain.
The mind works slower in this stunned landscape
of gloomy vistas and smudgy clouds, a dense
crust of sky, a world with a heart of stone.

A kind of day I have known since childhood
when the mind stumbles in its own mist, objects
lose their meaning and disturb like a nagging question.
Each day I walk to the top of a hill. Each
year it's steeper. But so long as I move,
therefore I am. The rain pelts down,
the wind escalates and pulls back my coat.

Gravity never lets me forget I'm subject
to earth. Climbing this muddy slope, the poise
of the inner ear helps keep me from slipping.
The day unfolds to the rhythm of breathing and the beat
of rain. My legs tingle with messages.
Who is this stooped, grey-haired old man
who bears my name? The person I am becoming.

I remember a long climb, once, that brought me
to the sight of a sea seething with energies,
a space of open possibility, whose depth could not
be guessed, a massive presence, deceptively clear
yet challenging the mind to grasp it fully.
Our senses play only with surfaces, eating
the look and sound of things. Trying to make
more of the world is like staring into deep water
and seeing nothing but your own face.

There are times I feel I'm exploring an unfamiliar
planet, treading gingerly, sniffing the atmosphere,
unable to name the flora or construe the signs,
nerves and senses on edge, an expendable robot
rummaging through a landscape that is not mine,
not rational, and not friendly. But before
the last batteries run out, this scout
will report to base: This is the world I saw.

10

THIRD WALK

The autumn sun is fierce – with ample fuel
for now, making light as we make
thought. What would be the thoughts of a sun?
This corner of the earth seems pleased
with itself today. A simple glass vase
on a window ledge is a rainbow zigzag
of light. Patterns of mould mottle a fencepost.
A bare but shapely tree has scattered a patchwork
of leaves through the wild grass. Puddles
glisten in the sun and footsteps trigger ripples.
The world is pure pleasure in the bristle of its textures.
For once its meaning seems sure and self-sufficient.

A cyclist spins past singing to herself.
A kid on the lawn plays a noisy game
with plastic toys. From inside an old house
the clatter of hammers and saws signals change.
A blind man taps his white cane.
A helicopter on crime patrol thrashes the air.
Outside the supermarket an old guitarist earns
a few coins but a manager chases him away.
Someone strolls along reading a book.
This is the dance of the species, each person
busy playing out their conception of the human,
focusing their willpower on the world.
Each mind seems to create a field of gravity
that curves space in its presence. Their thoughts
infiltrate the street and hover over houses:
a swarm of energy, a collective cloud of purpose.
Every thing seems made of the world yet wrapped
in mind like a transparent skin, more subtle than light.

I walk my shadow through a forest of shadows,
expressing myself as sign, as the figure of walking.
My silhouette slides over the concrete but leaves

no trace. With its foreshortened head and legs
it looks absurd, a cartoon of the human form,
then a ghost that vanishes behind a cloud.

2. CONSCIOUSNESS

Annihilating all that's made
To a green thought in a green shade.
—Andrew Marvell, 'The Garden'

Now you have gathered yourself together into yourself, see yourself
ending ahead of you in your own hands; you trace from time to time
with an uncertain gesture the outline of your face. And there is scarcely
any room inside you; and it almost calms you to think that nothing very
large can possibly abide in this narrowness; that even the stupendous must
become an inward thing and must restrict itself to fit the surroundings.
But outside, outside is beyond calculation.
—Rainer Maria Rilke

Consciousness is a fascinating but elusive phenomenon: it is impossible to
specify what it is, what it does, or why it evolved. Nothing worth reading
has been written about it.
—N.S. Sutherland

Studying consciousness was simply not the thing to do before you made
tenure, and even after you did it was looked upon with suspicion.
—Antonio Damasio

I shall often speak of [Descartes' theory that the mind and body are
separate] with deliberate abusiveness, as 'the dogma of the Ghost in the
Machine'. I hope to prove that it is entirely false, and false not in detail
but in principle. It is not merely an assemblage of particular mistakes. It
is one big mistake.
—Gilbert Ryle

Consciousness, then, is a great delusion. It arises through asking such
questions as 'Am I conscious now?' or 'What am I conscious of now?'

13

In that moment of questioning, an answer is concocted. . . . In this view only creatures capable of being so deluded could be conscious in the way that we human beings are. This probably means that humans are unique, or very nearly so, because only they have language, theory of mind, self-concept and all the other factors that help to create the delusion.

—Susan Blackmore

It is an interesting exercise to sit down and try to be conscious of what it means to say that consciousness does not exist.

—Julian Jaynes

Scientific psychology began in the nineteenth century as the study of the mind. The main technique was introspection, turning the mind inwards to examine what might be there. Not much was discovered, though, probably because the mind does not have access to most of what it actually does – just as a car engine, say, does not understand how it works.

—Michael C. Corballis

It is not possible to make consciousness visible by pointing to it from the outside because the act of pointing, of making explicit, is inside consciousness.

—Raymond Tallis

Consciousness is not something that happens inside us. It is something we do or make. Better: it is something we achieve. Consciousness is more like dancing than it is like digestion.

—Alva Noë

'I still remember,' continued Borgia, 'many years ago, in the Plaza de la Republica, there was an extraordinary traffic jam: all cars converged toward the obelisk, and nobody could move. Everyone was locked inside his car, and since it was quite cold, nobody opened the window. And then I thought: one thousand parallel consciousnesses are boiling inside each car, each raging inside its skull – there is a crowd of consciousnesses, but

there is no crowd – everyone's a prisoner sealed by walls higher than the obelisk. Because one consciousness and another can only touch the way two spheres can touch: just at one point – and even that one point may not be found.'
—Giulio Tononi

Another area of biology that some say lies beyond the limits of science is consciousness. Decades have passed without any real progress, says Russell Stannard, emeritus professor of physics at the Open University. . . . 'Consciousness is a very good candidate for us having exhausted all that can be said about it.'
—Michael Brooks

FIFTY NAMES

psyche, nous, συνείδηση (Greek), conscience, éveil (French), conocimiento, consciencia (Spanish), consapevolezza, coscienza (Italian), consciência (Portugese), сознание, самосознание (Russian), hinengaro (Māori), ىرایشوه (Persian), Bewusstsein, Wachheit (German), ge-wit (Anglo-Saxon), Chonaic (Irish), medvetande, uppmärksamhet (Swedish), bevidsthed (Danish), uvědomění, vědomí (Czech), tudat, átolvasás (Hungarian), teadvus (Estonian), bewussyn (Afrikaans), وعي (Arabic), malay (Filipino), 意識, 知覺 (Chinese), 의식 (Korean), tajunta (Finnish), העדות (Hebrew), bevissthet (Norwegian), meðvitund (Icelandic), fahamu (Swahili), روعش (Urdu), besef, bewustzijn (Dutch), ndërgjegje (Albanian), konsyans (Haitian), svijest (Croatian), kesedaran (Malay), iagona (Samoan), świadomość (Polish), 正気 (Japanese), உணர்வு (Tamil), animus, spiritus (Latin)

ONE HUNDRED DESCRIPTIONS

A speech balloon, a thought bubble.

A lake in which all things float as in the jelly of an eye.

A hissing, snake-like word with thirteen letters (one of which is 'I').

The ancient legacy of a meteor from an exoplanet.

A presence that saturates your body from the crown of your head to the soles of your feet.

A candle in a dark room, straining to illuminate the corners.

The Old Brain in the New Brain's arms.

Primal soup, bubbling.

The medium of all media.

Dark energy, whose existence is necessary but whose nature remains obscure.

Where it feels like what it feels like.

An alembic for the alchemy of turning grey matter into ideas and ideas into matter.

An instrument one spends a lifetime awkwardly learning to play.

A square peg in the round hole of the world.

A child of nature no longer willing to accept the authority of its parent.

A large window that can cloud over without warning and become a mirror.

A humbug, overrated like the prose that Molière's Bourgeois Gentleman discovers he has been speaking all his life.

A perennial flower blossoming in a landscape of flesh.

The headquarters of the hard problem.

The rationale for living with a single voice and a single name.

A wave function that hovers in uncertainty.

An observatory, a crow's nest, a periscope, a panopticon for surveillance.

A mansion teeming with ghosts and gremlins.

A mist with no taste or texture until mixed with the flavours of the world.

A cloud-chamber where thoughts collide, smash, exchange energy.

Mens mentis, the mind's mind.

A think-tank for pipe dreams, castle building, air guitar solos and thought experiments.

The panic room with the thickest walls.

The knife and fork for your meal of the world.

The tip of an iceberg which barely breaks the surface.

The state of which you are the only citizen, bordering the populous country whose noise vibrates all day in your ears.

A fundamental element, the companion to air, earth, fire, water.

The apparatus that takes particles and the spaces between them, and translates them into the street where you live.

A large room with small windows.

Evolution's favourite child and furthest advance, at least for the moment.

A sudden clearing at the heart of a cerebral labyrinth.

The lamp which bursts into light when you wake and you carry through the world all day.

An intricate, dangerous gift for which you still seek an operating manual.

A mercurial spill of awareness pouring over the surfaces of the world.

A black hole, a singularity.

A lush ambience you assume to be all yours, as air is taken for granted until the day you start gasping for breath.

Flashes of light from a rhythmic flux of waves.

A stomach in which to digest the sounds and shapes of words.

An essence that can never be bottled and sold in its pure form.

A mirror in which you see everything but yourself.

A dark, quiet corner in which you spin a web.

The eccentric conductor of a large orchestra.

A travelling salesman, office-seeker, beggar, evangelist, huckster.

An out-of-date system still stubbornly booting up.

The leftovers of dreams.

The world's only opportunity to make sense of itself.

The plaza where inside and outside mill together.

The agitation in the dark when you close your eyes.

Energy that knows itself as energy and uses its energy to know itself.

Mission central, head of the body politic.

An imperfect mechanism for remembering and naming the 10,000 things.

A presence, a present, that is renewed moment by moment.

The secret reservoir of greed, lust, envy and rage that you carry like a concealed suicide vest.

A lever straining to move the world.

The space inside the space inside your head.

Pandora's box, a gift you kick yourself for having opened.

The secret judge who hears, watches and condemns.

The launch pad for out-of-body experiences.

One of the billion bubbles in the sea at this moment.

Partner for an arranged marriage with the physical world.

Your personal microclimate with all its storms, pressure zones, and wayward currents of inner weather.

A brane, a weightless multiverse that overlaps with the gravity-laden world of flesh and blood.

A light that does not fade even when eyes fail.

The song of the ghost in the machine.

A parison, blown by the mind, that stretches out to swallow the world.

A rostrum to talk meaning into existence and the world into meaning.

A camera that can become screen, script, actor or audience.

A bottomless pool in which one floats or flounders.

A fragment of what one might imagine God to be, a piece He might mass-produce and scatter like seeds across planets.

The unbelievable lightness of thinking.

A room of your own, a bright, well-lit space, a studio free of rent.

The king's nervous taster.

A super-collider for a pilgrim to study the God particle.

The shoehorn that squeezes you into a world you do not fit.

Clouds of mental smoke from inside the head.

Games and distractions for solitary confinement.

A lone star, a single point of light in an expanding universe.

The ground under the ground, the eye inside the eye.

A fast-moving stream that carries a cargo of flotsam through your life.

A being made not of quarks or any substance but presence.

A magnetic storm in the brain, a noiseless tempest, an invisible whirlpool.

A delicate 40 hz mechanism whose equilibrium is endangered by alcohol, narcotics or passion.

A sun changeable but hard at work until the time it dissolves into ash.

The other side of the mirror, where physics becomes metaphysics.

A greenhouse in an adverse climate, shelter for the mind's fruits and flowers.

A cloud of sea mist caught in the beam of a lighthouse.

An iPhone permanently out of range.

A voracious gullet that swallows all things yet leaves them unchanged.

A scout engaged in the lonely task of reconnaissance, an avant-garde lone ranger.

A beehive busy with a ceaseless buzz and dance.

A priceless commodity recklessly squandered.

A miniature snow globe in which you see yourself in the snow holding an identical miniature snow globe.

A restless chameleon in the throes of metamorphosis.

A container without walls, a description without end.

The spawning grounds for a hundred images, none of which will survive for long yet each day breeds more.

3. BODY

What, indeed, does man know of himself! Can he even once perceive himself completely, laid out as if in an illuminated glass case? Does not nature keep much . . . from him, even about his body, to spellbind and confine him in a proud, deceptive consciousness, far from the coils of the intestines, the quick current of the blood stream, and the involved tremors of the fibres? She threw away the key; and woe to the calamitous curiosity which might peer just once through a crack.
—Friedrich Nietzsche

I have been living for some time amongst a people who are more or less directly the descendants of a culture and civilisation which was a contrary of that which we have known. . . . When I am rocked by the roads against any of them – kids, women, men – their flesh is most gentle, is granted, touch is in no sense anything but the natural law of flesh, there is none of that pull-away which, in the States, causes a man for all the years of his life the deepest sort of questioning of the rights of himself to the wild reachings of his own organism.
—Charles Olson

Acute consciousness of having a body – that is the absence of health . . . Which is as much as to say that I have never been well.
—E.M. Cioran

By and by, your attention becomes so intensely focused that you no longer notice the raw knuckles, the cramping thighs, the strain of maintaining nonstop concentration. A trance-like state settles over your efforts, the [mountain] climb becomes a clear-eyed dream. The accrued guilt and clutter of day-to-day existence, all of it is temporarily forgotten . . . crowded from your thoughts by an overpowering clarity of purpose, and by the seriousness of the task at hand.
—Jon Krakauer

Certainly music traverses our bodies in profound ways, putting an ear in the stomach, in the lungs, and so on. It knows all about waves and nervousness. But it involves our body, and bodies in general, in another element. It strips bodies of their inertia, of the materiality of their presence: it disembodies bodies.
—Gilles Deleuze

Tiny machines called ribosomes find and read the gene sentences and make them into something physical. Word is made flesh.
—Christopher Potter

Apart from feeling that my inside is a big black hole, dense enough to draw all light into it so that there appears a gap in the sky where I am supposed to be, yet, nevertheless others see light bouncing off me. They call my name. I answer 'What?' . . . Where, what, and how is my 'me,' my solid spatial physical me? Where's the jar on which to adhere the stick-on label 'Len Lye', my dear?
—Len Lye

Science tells us that we are merely beasts, but we don't feel like that. We feel like angels trapped inside the bodies of beasts, forever craving transcendence.
—Vilayanur S. Ramachandran

I envisage our brains will eventually complete their epic journey from the obsolete human bodies they have inhabited for millions of years and, through the use of bidirectional, thought-driven interfaces, operate a myriad of nanotools that will serve as our new eyes, ears and hands in the many tiny worlds of nature.
—Miguel A.L. Nicolelis

If I feel disoriented, light-headed, awry,
my hand reaches for the edge of this heavy table
as a refuge, cool and dense, a place to anchor.
But what to make of this haywire tangle of veins,
this wrinkled landscape of skin, this maze of fingertip
loops and ridges that are my signature? The body
manifests and defines my boundaries, but baffles
as an opaque world lodged in an opaque world,
the jar that holds the essence of my mind.

That is a mind's-eye-view, and how
could it not be when words are the mind's calling?
Yet how could it continue to write if not hand
in hand with the body, eyes and fingertips as medium,
ghost ideas materialising out of thin air?

It would be simpler if body and mind were not
an odd couple, a de facto marriage of opposites.
Only the body is bound by the laws of physics
and dimensions of space. And only the mind agonises
over their relationship. Until their final meeting
on a dissection table, they share the same breath,
partners in an arranged marriage that begins at birth,
intimate, codependent, complementary, yet often conflicted.
The body and mind maintain a dialogue for life,
yet each has its own private monologue, capable
of ending in tragic illness or impulsive suicide.

The weight of limbs, the tingle of nerves – could
such details have been different? The world you inherit
is yours to give away but never to exchange,
with all its daily rituals of maintenance – washing
and drying the surfaces of yourself, like washing and drying
the dishes – through decades of cut hair, nails,
dead skin, sweat, urine and blood,
keeping up standards, warding off entropy.

The mind sings, the body supplies the beat.
Bass to the mind's treble, continuo to its recitative.
The heart keeps pumping blood, ostinato,
the pulse and lungs rarely skip a bar,
and countless cells renew themselves like clockwork.
Somehow the mind conducts this seething dance.
This music targets the nervous system
and the less the dancers think, the better they move.

At the gym the heart beats faster for an hour.
The mind allows the body to do the talking:
a noisy monologue of gesture and sensation.
All the mind can contribute is keeping track
of numbers, though it's also free to admire
other bodies – lithe, muscled or shapely.
The goal is to persevere. 'I sweat, therefore I am.'
Up the mountain at a centre for extreme sports
contestants sharpen their senses, every sinew
focused on the task of finishing alive and first.
This player says, 'Dancing with death is my thing.'
There are still some bones he hasn't broken.

Sex has its own assured aesthetic,
its own way to read the world, in the blood,
clandestine and quick as lightning as it appraises endless
variations on the human form. When light and shade
contour a body, your own body responds,
a lode of feelings to mine or to keep secret.

Desire can be a torment, but it is also a means
of giving the body its due, its just deserts.
The mind and body seldom coincide except
when sex coaches you in carnal knowledge.
Even philosophers do it, though practice keeps
pressing them to rethink their theories. Skin
to skin, blazing with natural forces, lovers
concentrate as their world narrows to the senses.

25

Nostrils inhale the salty flavours of skin,
the ripe, musky scent of lovemaking
in sheets rumpled and moist with its juices.
Pleasure entails the mischief and fever of carnival
and while the body brought you here, you
and your partner created this space by imagination,
by a meeting of minds and pact for mutual pleasure.
For some the act falls short of its promise
yet they are always drawn back to this ancient
dance which celebrates the body and sounds its energy.

There are other crucial matters to discuss such as love
and conception, but they open onto huge landscapes,
and now your own body is slipping out of order,
issuing warnings in a language you struggle to interpret.
Now you can't disown your flesh and protest
I'm not sick, it's only my body! A mind
also trembles when limbs shake with fever.

I have shivered from the frost of cancer spreading in silence
and darkness, freezing my energy. To eat, sleep,
think became a struggle and I blamed the body
for double-crossing me. Then I realised the enemy
was a trespasser who threatened us both, and my flesh
was fighting its own last-ditch battle.
Together we were raw recruits, quarrelsome comrades,
until the invader was torn out by the knife; then scarred
but sewn up, we could resume our old partnership.

No thought without a body – that's
the deal. Your senses are wired to the world. Avatar,
you strive to fit its fabric snug as a glove.
That we are dressed in flesh with brains of meat
rather than metal adds the colours and flavours
of a chaos that no robot or algorithm can know.
Body nestles against body, sharing warmth
in creature comfort. Swimming in the intricacy of flesh
is our personal terroir, the ground of our ideas.

26

4. LANGUAGE

Languages are something of a mess. . . . [John] Quijada wrote that his 'greater goal' was 'to attempt the creation of what human beings, left to their own devices, would never create naturally, but rather only by conscious intellectual effort: an idealised language whose aim is the highest possible degree of logic, efficiency, detail, and accuracy in cognitive expression.
—Joshua Foer

What a sentence means, and what it refers to, lack the properties that something typically needs in order to make a difference in the world. The information conveyed by this sentence has no mass, no momentum, no electric charge, no solidity, and no clear extension in the space within you, around you, or anywhere.
—Terence W. Deacon

The kind of poem I produced in those days was hardly anything more than a sign I made of being alive, of passing or having passed, or hoping to pass, through certain intense human emotions. It was a phenomenon of orientation rather than of art, thus comparable to stripes of paint on a roadside rock or to a pillared heap of stones marking a mountain trail. But then, in a sense, all poetry is positional: to try to express one's position in regard to the universe embraced by consciousness, is an immemorial urge.
—Vladimir Nabokov

For a man's problem, the moment he takes speech up in all its fullness, is to give his work his seriousness, a seriousness sufficient to cause the thing he makes to try to take its place alongside the things of nature.
—Charles Olson

Look hard at nature. It is in the nature
of things to look, and look back, harder.
Botany is panic of another description.
—Allen Curnow, 'There Is a Pleasure in the Pathless Woods'

Flowers, dew, stars, skies . . . the words ruled, you see; they held the keys of the kingdom, and I did not realise until I had spent a few more years growing and observing that the kingdom which glorified those words was as much a prison as my grey serge tunic and knotted tie and lace-up black shoes.
—Janet Frame

Animals in the wild simply do not have much to communicate about. Most animal communications seem to consist either of single signals or of random variations on a theme, as in the case of birdsong. If we suppose that animals communicate to signal events to one another, such as the dangerous presence of a snake, then a single signal will generally be sufficient, and will have the advantage of economy.
—Michael C. Corballis

I fully agree with Schopenhauer when he writes, 'Thoughts die the moment they are embodied by words'.
—Jacques Hadamard

Niels Bohr, in conversation with [Werner] Heisenberg, remarked: 'When it comes to atoms, language can be used only as poetry. The poet too is not nearly so concerned with describing facts as with creating images.'
—Nick Laird

Music is arguably the most direct and unfettered expression of mortality and how we deal with it. What music can utter, words and the structures they entail can only disguise.
—Robin Maconie

THE DAYBOOK

A table and a quiet corner revive the dream
of authorship, with a Hi-Tec pen and a 'Big
Ideas' notebook from the Three Dollar Shop.
Now it's my turn to try to make sense,
to add a new crust of words to the pentimento,
to log some casual expressions of the lust
for language, the itch to write, *cacoëthes scribendi*.

                              *

Writing is like walking, wandering along a line,
though I often pause to retrace a step. I know
my footprints are transient but somehow the unhurried
journey focuses the mind and steadies the hand.
The ink of earlier daybooks has dried and faded,
the imprint of my passage through time – cup circles,
sweat smudges, shopping lists, New
Year's resolutions. Without a recording angel
to register my lifetime of mistakes and misspeakings, this
is my avatar, a lucky find one day
for an alien archaeologist poking through our ruins.
Another reason to write as if it matters.

                              *

When I walk at night, I see each brightly
lit window as a mind at work. Once
when I glimpsed bookshelves, paintings, and an old man
writing, I fantasised that a great avant-garde
émigré lived secretly in my suburb. Tonight
I pass a writer bathed in the glow of a computer.
Whatever he's writing – and it may be best not
to ask – my older, less innocent eyes
still find this figure hopeful and mysterious.

*

How in language to describe the sudden collapse
when words lose their power and are reduced
to dreary platitudes, an empty buzz of sound?
Hungry for meaning, we want words to bathe
nature in their light, but sometimes they burn down
to a pile of black clinkers in an opaque world.

*

Now too tired to work, I will simply
listen to music, the most credible of languages.
I wrap its sound round me like the warmth of a coat.
Music is opulent but abstract, not obsessed
with representation as words are. A close-fitting chain
of notes gifts its sense of order to the world.

*

These long-distance writers are a curious breed,
high-strung, obsessive, welcoming solitary confinement,
yet never certain their idea or talent will last
the distance. Writing is such an anxious job they're desperate
for rituals, and many prefer the ancient custom
of writing words by hand to the rote pounding
on a keyboard. My own tactile, fetish instrument
for this black art is a liquid ink pen,
which is bad news for clothes. Other writers
swear by pencils. Thoreau even invented
an improved pencil. Writers also get addicted
to clipboards, legal pads, or background music.
A copy of Roget's Thesaurus and a fat dictionary
reassure by arming them with a vast arsenal.
Their craft is a thankless compulsion but as bold as alchemy,
a secret process to match the legendary philosopher's
stone by turning leaden language into gold.

30

Surfacing after long immersion in an editing job
and hurrying to a public event, I suffer from the bends.
The reception is a space awash with talk,
splashing off walls and floor. I do my best to float
but the flood of conversation, the whirlpool of words leave
me waterlogged and spluttering. Quiet is a distant shore.

*

My friend the poet has migraines. His comments grow
increasingly lateral. His wife insists on a scan
which tragically reveals a tumour inside his brain.
I visit him soon after surgery. He is fascinated
by curious details but lacks the words to explain.
His family is desperate to share the strange insights
that lie behind his urgent, frustrated gestures.

*

This concert offers calm, clear music
creating a room where details have place and purpose,
square-built with a serene rightness. But now
a different music breaks in, which unsettles
by its odd angles and sudden spasms, its unpredictable
stops and starts, its changes that outpace thought.
Each variation is another stab at a password,
always incomplete, but the search for the code continues,
refusing to take the language of music for granted.

*

The writer's fear of the half-finished manuscript:
he longs for words that grip as an equation can,
but the more articulate he becomes, the less confident

he feels that a perfect language is not a mirage.
Using words is as basic to living as breathing,
but sometimes words seem merely to gossip
about other words as all they care to do.
Here is a colony of ants on the page, a maze
of shadows cast by thought, tangled strands
like algae or sea lace quivering in the currents,
the myriad debris of an explosion in a language factory.

*

My friend the Professor of Philosophy is writing a book
about weighty questions like 'Why is there something
rather than nothing?' or 'What is the meaning of life?'
His razor-sharp mind and logical training
will expose them as tautologies, gibberish, pseudo-questions.
He is offended by all forms of untidy prose.
My murky mind is sanitised briefly by his acid.

*

All thinking is wishful, all questions are rhetorical
with implied quote marks. There's no escape
from double talk. But talk is cheap and so we try
again, wired with the need to name, to relate
our lives. I think, therefore I write on the walls
of our cave. A word is a thought experiment,
a lamp rubbed to summon the genie of the world.
It yields a flash of sense, the prize of a moment
in focus, then decays to a clump of letters,
obscure sounds, an enigmatic pattern of pixels.
Nobody steps twice into the same word.

*

Connoisseurs of cool irony, the artists of our sceptical
age distance themselves from beauty and directness.

Occasionally a poet will play with fire by sneaking in
a few subtle, ambivalent hints of the sublime.
But wait, here's an old band from the sixties,
their electric guitars still screaming and cursing
and their lyrics dense as a black hole, whipping up
an almost convincing version of existential angst.
The drummer attacks everything in reach and the thumping
bass makes bodies vibrate. Swaying, I respond
to something old and elemental in this defiant
stereotype, this out-of-fashion swagger of seriousness.

5. MELANCHOLIA

I went to the radio interview
But I ended up alone
At the microphone.
—Neil Young, 'On the Beach'

I had my first conscious feeling of an outside sadness, or it seemed to come from outside, from the sound of the wind moaning in the wires. I looked up and down the white dusty road and saw no one. The wind was blowing from place to place past us, and I was there, in between, listening. I felt a burden of sadness and loneliness as if something had happened or begun and I knew about it. I don't think I had yet thought of myself as a person looking out at the world; until then, I felt I was the world.
—Janet Frame

In young people, if for the rest they have a tendency to δυσκολια [difficulty or discontent], ill humours and annoyances of a personal kind are wont readily to take on a general character. . . . To fashion for myself a suitable life of my own was my effort from morning till night. . . . The need to know oneself, even to gnaw at oneself, laid a powerful hold on me. . . . A nervous irritability overcame me, and who knows to what length of folly I might not have proceeded, had not the enticements of life, of vanity, and the compulsion of regular studies worked in the opposite direction.
—Friedrich Nietzsche

The feeling that life is essentially inadequate to the human spirit, and yet that a good life must avoid saying so, is naturally at home with most versions of pastoral; in pastoral you take a limited life and pretend it is the full and normal one, and a suggestion that one must do this with all life, because the normal is itself limited, is easily put into the trick. . . .
—William Empson

. . . first and last things often tend to have an adolescent note – unless, possibly, they are directed by some venerable and rigid religion. Nature expects a full-grown man to accept the two black voids, fore and aft [of his life], as stolidly as he accepts the extraordinary visions in between. Imagination, the supreme delight of the immortal and the immature, should be limited. . . . I rebel against this state of affairs. I feel the urge to take my rebellion outside and picket nature.
—Vladimir Nabokov

[Nabokov] has remarked . . . that only a single letter divides the comic from the cosmic.
—Brian Boyd

Genuine boredom has not yet arrived if we are merely bored with this book or that movie, with this job or that idle moment. Genuine boredom occurs when one's whole world is boring. Then abysmal boredom, like a muffling fog, drifts where it will in the depths of our openness, sucking everything and everyone, and ourselves along with them, into a numbing sameness. This kind of boredom reveals what is in terms of a whole.
—Martin Heidegger

. . . he just wants to lie in the sand and breathe.
He has nothing in common with the world.
He feels like a handle broken off a jug,
but the jug doesn't know it's broken and keeps going to the well. . . .
Thick and heavy as glue *sunt lacrimae rerum.*
But all that's only background, incidental.
Within him, there's awful darkness, in the darkness a small boy.
God of humour, do something about him, OK?
God of humour, do something about him today.
—Wisława Szymborska, 'A Film from the Sixties'

Lacrimae rerum, absurdity, otherness, angst,
Alienation, ostranie, strangeness, acedia, anomie,
Tristitia, nausée, duende, taska, skushno,
Saudade, wabi sabi, amertume, tristesse,
Anhedonia, mal de siècle, Weltschmerz, melancholia.

A four-year-old seething with energies,
his mind a building site dangerous to enter.
When does he learn to read? Or first puzzle
over his mirror image, repeating his given name
until it loses meaning and his face is a stranger?
He lies in bed, floating in space and darkness,
sensing a strange depth, as dizzy as peering
down a well which seems never to end.

A crowd sweeps him away from his mother. To the lost
child, streets are endless, sounds startle.
He discovers the cold panic of being alone.
At night he listens to his heart beat in counterpoint
to his breathing. Diastole, systole – a bass drum,
a private performance that echoes through his body,
his measure, his time signature, learned by heart.
He considers his breath and wonders what will protect
its rhythm when he is asleep. As a test he stops
as long as he can. But as the stillness and deadness grow,
he takes fright, splutters to breathe again.

Exploring the hills on a summer morning, he begins
playfully to run, but the slope drops steeply
and suddenly his feet belong to the hill, his body
out of control racing breathlessly down
until gravity hurls him over his heels into darkness.

Soon he is old enough to throw stones
at birds, until his favourite uncle catches
and punishes him. In his hurt and anger, the idea
that other forms of life are capable of feeling
pain penetrates his thinking for the first time.

Later he cries when confronted by his uncle's face
under a grotesque mask, his eyes closed
and struggling to breathe. This is the boy's first death.

Wandering through the gardens of an old house
in the magic light of a low sun he samples
the scent of pine with its roughness and sap, the peppery
aroma of mint, the lush fragrance of honeysuckle.
His mind blossoms and for the first time he fathoms
the happiness of being alone in a sensuous world.

Books are another space he adopts as home
with their vivid clusters of words, like gardens neatly
planted; the smells of paper, ink and glue
are winding paths for visitors to lose themselves.

A small girl his age comes to visit.
They play on tricycles, then to his surprise and delight
she whispers the idea of exploring the basement. Giggling
in the dim light, they shed their clothes, absorbed
in the mystery of bodies. Then they hear his mother
shouting: 'Where are you? What are you doing?'
Burning with guilt they rush to cover themselves.

The first time he feels ice in his veins
is the day two older boys grab him
on the railway bridge and force him, kicking
and crying, to the edge as the train roars up. Every
cell in his body screams with the urge to survive.
Then he's engulfed in thunder and smoke and pulled
back up, deafened and choking but alive,
free to flee as the boys howl with laughter.

Years pass and he reaches adolescence, but the climate
of his mind is unsettled and overcast, his days
spent reading in a small, dark bedroom.
He feels he has little in common with his parents.

They love him in their way, but they are adults
who never question things. If they had reasons
for creating a child, their meaning is not his.
He hates the taken-for-granted family rituals.
He is dreamy and self-righteous, riddled with a stubborn
confusion. Then one day he is seized by the thought
that God really exists and sees everything.
How can his parents be so casual, reducing God
to a Sunday routine? Avidly he seizes on religion
as the answer, though its requirements are huge and absolute.

Baffled, his parents watch as he overloads his days
with bible study and meditation and prayer. He struggles
to overcome his fear of being found wanting.
But in two years his fervour burns itself out.
He finds God's ministers smug and impatient
with the problems he raises. Born again to the secular
world, he makes an effort to be more relaxed
and social, keeping his cargo of darkness to himself.
Yet he is shy in company and cannot find
a girl eager to share serious thoughts.
Clumsy at sport, unsure of his body, his mind
goes blank when teased by his peers. He is only happy
when left alone to read, think and dream.

Like a shoehorn, a mind is meant to ease you
into the world, but his makes a poor fit.
His surroundings are safe but ugly and bland, and his hunger
for meaning is more urgent than the cry of his hormones.

He is called a spoiled brat, teased for earnestness,
mocked for his moods and ordered to lighten up.
He takes refuge in his head, but stewing too often
in his own juices turns his thoughts sour.
Yet his anger is directed not at other people
but at his own situation, sealed in a body
and hemmed in by the stifling presence of the world.

The prosaic ritual of washing the family dishes
turns serious one night as he dries
the ugliest of knives. No longer a good
son, his hands weigh up this razor-sharp
blade for his own secret use. Somehow
he manages to place it back in its sheath on the wall.

Daily he walks to school over a long bridge
and cannot resist pausing at the highest point.
The bridge casts a graceful arc of shadow
through which cars speed. His body sizes up
the plunge, hungry as an arrow lining up its target.
Balancing on the spur of the moment, he stares into space
in conversation with nothing. Curiosity competes with the surge
of fear in his stomach. At last, clutching his bag
he forces his legs to move, like a parent wrenching
his child away from the forbidden, to the end of the bridge.
This daily meditation leaves him no wiser.

He searches libraries for a writer who shares his obsessions.
He is jubilant when a book begins: 'There is but one
truly serious philosophical question and that is suicide.'
So obvious a challenge, but few have dared to raise it –
and this writer is still alive! He cries when he hears
of Camus's accidental death in a car crash.

All of this happened a long time ago,
before the internet, before sombre teenage
songs could reassure him he wasn't the only oddball.
Still, he survived his dark time, not merely
drifting through it but resolving to accept his life.
Everything has followed from that knife-edge choice.
He has grown thicker skin, and learned to move
between his reality and theirs. He has developed
a keen eye for the colours and textures of the world,
and known the mystery of happiness flooding the heart.
Once his father carried him on his shoulders,
now his mind has learned to carry itself.

Yet darkness still seeps through the cracks
and strangeness returns in ambush. A life is a fragile
framework, the mind can find itself in free
fall, and even a small riddle can lead
him back to the old enigma of an opaque world.
At such times he must devise his own escape,
scrambling back to the haven of common sense.

A child learns to conquer his fear of the dark:
surely an adult can develop *savoir faire*?
But for him the world will always retain an odd
ambience, a taint of the arbitrary, mysteries not solved
but shelved. And later, when death comes to deliver
some meaningless ending, he'll be engulfed by the old quandaries.

6. SELF

Life first arose out of self-organising molecules.
—Christopher Potter

What is the work of works for man if not to establish, in and by each one of us, an absolutely original centre in which the universe reflects itself in a unique and inimitable way?
—Pierre Teilhard de Chardin

[The atom] enters the bloodstream, knocks at the door of a nerve cell, enters, and supplants the carbon that was part of it. The cell belongs to a brain and it is my brain; the cell in question, and within it the atom in question, are in charge of my writing, in a mysterious game that nobody has yet described. It . . . guides this hand of mine to impress on this paper this dot here, this one.
—Primo Levi

As a rule, New Zealanders are not known for being introspective. They are modest, outward-looking people who live in big landscapes, and most of them probably find American-style self-examination to be a bit narcissistic, though they are far too polite to say so.
—Carl Elliott

I no more wrote than read the book which is
The self I am
—Delmore Schwartz, 'I am a Book I neither Wrote nor Read'

Suddenly I was alone . . . I felt, that afternoon of my childhood, that a very serious event had just occurred. It was my first awakening, the first indication, the premonitory sign of consciousness. Before that I had been only a being. From that moment, I was more and less than that. Each self begins with a rift and a revelation.
—E.M. Cioran

41

The Western conception of the person as a bounded, unique, more or less integrated motivational and cognitive universe, a dynamic centre of awareness, emotion, judgement, and action, organised into a distinctive whole and set constrastively against other such wholes is, however incorrigible it may seem to us, a rather peculiar idea within the context of the world's cultures.
—Clifford Geertz

I'm really just a little window on a lovely machinery that's doing lots of things.
—Daniel Wegner

The PSM [phenomenal self-model] of Homo sapiens is probably one of nature's best inventions. It is an efficient way to allow a biological organism to consciously conceive of itself (and others) as a whole. Thus it enables the organism to interact with its internal world as well as with the external environment in an intelligent and holistic manner.
—Thomas Metzinger

Man at his peril breaks the full circuit of object, image, action at any point. The meeting edge of man and the world is also his cutting edge. . . . If he stays fresh at the coming in, he will be fresh at his going out.
—Charles Olson

It camps in the Rocky Mountains of the skull.
An eternal refugee. It is I and I,
with the fearful hope that I have found at last
a friend, am it. But the self
is so lonely, so distrustful that it does not
accept anyone, even me.
—Adam Zagajewski, 'The Self'

Mind and behaviour are the moment-to-moment results of the operation of galaxies of nuclei and cortical parcels articulated by convergent and

divergent neural projections. If the galaxies are well organised and work harmoniously, the owner makes poetry. If not, madness ensues.
—Antonio Damasio

To study the self is to forget the self. To forget the self is to be enlightened by all things of the universe. To be enlightened by all things of the universe is to cast off the body and mind of the self as well as those of others.
—13th-century Japanese Zen master Dogen

Tell me, why is it hard
To make arrangements with yourself?
—Neil Young, 'Tell Me Why'

A-list celebrities in their gated media communities
smile down at us from the summit of selfhood, like a teaser
trailer for the next stage in human evolution.
Yet non-celebrities also have their self-importance,
their image and brand to keep ship-shape.
No red-carpet fashions, no paparazzi or airbrushing
but the challenge of maintenance is no less complex.

To keep it manageable I like to think of my self
as a stick figure wandering the world, *Homo
erectus*, capital I – that ancient symbol,
worn off my keyboard, oddly simple and singular
compared with the hundred different words for snow.
The French have *je*, the Spanish *yo*, which are also
stick figures. Consider the adventures of I,
yours or mine, like a favourite cartoon strip
published each morning. In a city of stick
figures, ours with luck will go on stepping
from one panel to the next, an animated pictogram,
able also to emit some simple speech
balloons and emoticons of the smiley or grimacing kind,
a slapstick cartoon character, a self streamlined

to fit the black-and-white world of the commonplace.
Sometimes the tiny figure bears a bag on its back
like a vagrant who lugs round his whole life
an archaeology of empty bottles and found objects.
My cargo is close to bursting – years of sights
and smells, ideas and anxieties, mistakes and regrets –
but for the moment I'm still mobile, still fossicking.
Meanwhile, since Rimbaud wrote *je est*
un autre, artists and scientists see the self
as worse than a cartoon character – it's an illusion,
a miasma coiling up from the stream of consciousness,
the buzz of a billion neurons blurring into one,
a phantom conjured by language. Still, this
is a friendly and familiar ghost, a loyal factotum.
Call it a dirty job but someone's got
to do it. Granted, this stick figure footman
has to be allowed at least a ten percent
chaos factor for broken china, missed
deadlines, lost keys and slips of the tongue.

This afternoon I visit someone in a nursing home
who sadly has exhausted his legal chaos quota.
The last time Brian drove, two years ago,
he lost his way, parked somewhere, went shopping,
then forgot the car. His sons have since sold it
and his unkempt house. Angrily he insists he's still
able. *Able was I ere I saw Elba.*
Now he's exiled to this island, a rest home
of 'holistic care' for selves as frail as eggshells
who need help to bathe, dress, walk
and sort their pills (rivalling the stars in antidepressants).

At 90 my relative lives mostly in the past,
especially his war years. Conversations lock themselves
in a spiral because his short-term memory
keeps shrinking and news must be repeated. His world
is constantly renewed but seems to him incomplete.

44

He is angry that his grandchildren 'never visit'.
But who has left those photos and chocolates?
He confuses everyone's name, and when he strides
off with his walker to patrol the corridors, he gets lost.
His self has shrunk but he is still full of raucous energy
unlike his neighbours who nap quietly in the day room.
He tells rude stories and reverts to the cynical
black humour of a man on the front lines.

Now that no elixir can unravel his dementia,
his snarled strands of self, is there no
compensation? Isn't he glad to be free of the drudgery
of a job, the rules of politeness, the demands of persona?
As case histories suggest, some strange
energies are released when certain neurites die.
A woman becomes so aware of subtle change
that her world is a dizzy turbulence like a painting
whose colours keep running. A man with heightened
hearing inhabits a seething ambience of sirens,
explosions, panting lungs. Here Rimbaud would feel
at home, but my relative thinks he's back in the war.

I'm exhausted, and dinnertime offers an excuse
to slip away. As bibs are tied round necks,
all the residents perk up, except for the few
for whom survival is a sentence of hard labour.

I leave the rest home, determined to invent
some other way to grow old. I jaywalk
across the street to catch a bus, confident
that my nervous system will keep my body clear
of the fast cars. Safely on board I join
twenty quiet heads, some dozing after
their day's work, killing time like the elderly
alone with their favourite fantasies or anxieties
but the mood is very different – these are travellers
in the midst of their lives, still soundly self-possessed.

Fingers are busy tapping out texts
or flipping pages. A woman peruses a magazine
of celebrity gossip, another is deep into a self-help
bestseller about how to crash the rich list.

The self is the vehicle of our lives, a complex, rickety
contraption often with a mind of its own. Impatient
to go places, it is always on the hustle,
prodding us to start a family, a business, a film,
some enterprise that will involve a tumult of choices,
arguments, money worries, insecurities, frustrations,
friends neglected, too much coffee and booze.
So long as he can, the stick figure continues
to deliver the goods, leaving in his wake a lifetime
of projects and fiascoes loosely linked by his name
as he staggers along from one page to the next.

The boundaries of the last panel are reached when a life
becomes a story at a funeral, freezing the first
into the third person. As friends we gather to celebrate
a fellow self and grant our veteran fifteen
minutes of fame. But sadly his cloud of consciousness,
his haze of surprise and possibility have now evaporated
leaving only his symbol, a cartoon mask.

7. MICRO / MACRO

The universe may
Be as large as they say,
But it wouldn't be missed
If it didn't exist.
—Piet Hein

This ultimate stock we have devised to name
Procreant atoms, matter, seeds of things,
Or primal bodies, as primal to the world.
—Lucretius

And he showed me more, a little thing, the size of a hazelnut, on the palm of my hand, round like a ball. I looked at it thoughtfully and wondered, 'What is this?' and the answer came: 'It is all that is made.' I marvelled that it continued to exist and did not suddenly disintegrate; it was so small.
—Julian of Norwich (c. 1400)

The fluctuations from which clusters and superclusters form, and the even vaster ones spread right across the sky . . . are the outcome of microscopic quantum processes at an ultra-ancient epoch when the universe was squeezed smaller than a golfball.
—Martin Rees

A well-known feature of quantum fields in ordinary, empty, uncurved spacetime is that their jitters allow pairs of particles . . . to momentarily erupt out of the nothingness, live briefly, and then smash into each other, with mutual annihilation the result.
—Brian Greene

The universe seems to be a machine for processing information made out of some 10^{80} visible particles.
—Christopher Potter

There are lots of concepts where the surface features of the phenomena are more interesting than the microstructure. Consider mud or Beethoven's Ninth Symphony. Mud behaviour is molecular behaviour but that is not the interesting thing about mud.

—John R. Searle

The mind . . . works on the data it receives very much as a sculptor works on his block of stone. We may, if we like, by our reasonings unwind things back to that black and jointless continuity of space and moving clouds of swarming atoms which science calls the only real world. But all the while the world we live and feel in will be that which our ancestors and we . . . have extricated out of this, like sculptors, by simply rejecting certain portions of the given stuff. Other sculptors, other statues from the same stone! Other minds, other worlds from the same monotonous and inexpressive chaos!

—William James

To get a sense of them [the mystics], imagine a Hernando Cortez in the middle of an invisible geography. . . . For mysticism is an adventure, a vertical adventure: it forays upward and seizes another form of space.

—E.M. Cioran

> The building trembles and objects rattle. Whatever
> is happening has my full attention. More tremors,
> then stillness. Only a minor shock today
> but a reminder that this restless earth has no sympathy
> for our human foothold. Meanwhile the sun continues
> silently to shine, keeping its thermonuclear health
> confidential, and the sky reserves comment on its own
> deep-seated problems. People return to work.
>
> Our personal world can seem staid and immovable,
> but to science everything is unsettled, not just the crust.
> Take an elevator to the basement at the speed of light
> and step out into a crazy quantum field

of particles flitting in and out of existence,
or head for the top floor where space curves,
stars explode and black holes devour.
As John Keats put it, 'Uproar's your only music.'

At lunchtime I pass a prophet of doom whose placard
thunders warnings of a giant asteroid from an Aztec
stone calendar. I have many worries
but I'll wager that the earth will outlast this afternoon,
that my car will still be standing where I parked it,
and my wife will join me to share an evening meal.
The odds are good for the best of possible worlds.

But now here's another tremor. The light trembles
and shadows dance to the deep vibrations of the earth.

Soon the buildings stop quivering. Scientists
can return to their labs and their search for terra firma.
Everyone would prefer a world with a firm ceiling
and floor, but always the ground falls away
into uncertainty and there is no end to the sky,
only expansion – quarks and neutrinos, asteroids,
galaxies and multiverses, all in ceaseless movement.

We have learned to grow or shrink like Alice
or to imitate Maxwell's Demon, sharper than a needle
and smaller than a grain of sand, who can slam-dunk
particles like basketballs. From nanometres to parsecs, from
        nanoseconds
to chiliads, we humans have become ubiquitous.
But we no longer reside at the heart of things.
We lack tūrangawaewae, a firm place to stand.

                    *

How to elude vertigo? By sleight of hand,
retreating to our human scale, our human senses.

The daily ground we inhabit is solid as common
sense, our human version of the strong force
which allows us with deceptive ease to step across
a billion jittery atoms, like the water in constant
motion under this steadfast bridge I stride
across each day without a flicker of misgiving.

We live inside the rainbow. The objects our eyes
make tangible may be mere dreams and guesses,
castles in the air, but we know their textures
intimately. Visiting a former house, my fingers
touch the banister and remember gripping this piece
of wood as a child. The pictures the senses paint
so plausibly conjure up the freshness of air after
rain, the coolness of wet grass, the mulch
of leaves, the pungent smell of wood smoke,
the drone of a plane from a bank of clouds.
We make a life, we make a world. The shimmering
particles cohere, like this stone grasped in my hand,
or my fingers themselves. When a wave function
collapses, it escapes from nowhere and joins our zone,
assumes colour and flavour, entangled with the wind
and sunlight of our familiar turf, our middle earth,
salvaged high and dry from the quantum sea.

A human being is a boatload of a billion cells,
a luxury liner under full sail. Brainwaves
pulse steadily, keeping my neurons in sync
and my thoughts afloat. Thankfully all seem dedicated
to survival, and my crew and I ride out the storms.
Macro and micro mesh, the one and the many.
Their seafaring ways remain an enigma, but I'm
a grateful captain and there are no signs of mutiny yet.

*

How to grasp inhuman scale? Our tightest
grip is mathematics, our ideal code is symmetry.

50

If only atoms up close were perfect twins
to the spinning galaxies, it would confirm the dream
of an ordered cosmos – but sadly that mirage melts.
Yet we can still see the atom as our ancestor,
the first seed in our nuclear family.
Somehow nature was born from its primal dance
of energy. Presaging life, it moved and changed
in response to surroundings, attracted or repelled, bonded
and entangled, until coming to a violent end.
Atoms are how the world hangs together
and why we are also here, creating
a strange kinship or whakapapa across the millennia.
By countless tiny steps atoms learned
to unite and become smart energy like the sap
of plants. Atoms to molecules to cells – a dizzy
climb – and a ladder that extends beyond us.

8. SLEEPING AND WAKING

Life is really more fun when you are not conscious of it.
—Tor Nørretranders

Every human being is fully an artist when creating the worlds of dream, and the lovely semblance of dream is the precondition of all the arts of image-making. . . . A person with artistic sensibility relates to the reality of dream in the same way a philosopher relates to the reality of existence: he attends to it closely and with pleasure, using these images to interpret life, and practising for life with the help of these events.
—Friedrich Nietzsche

The simple self at the bottom of the mind is a lot like music but not yet poetry.
—Antonio Damasio

. . . in dreams we are not only perceptually and emotionally hyper-conscious but cognitively deficient and off-line to sensory inputs and motor outputs. That is to say, we are anesthetised and paralysed in addition to being hallucinated, emotional, disoriented, and amnesic.
—J. Allan Hobson

All species that have been studied in detail appear to sleep, whether reptiles, birds or mammals. [Yet] there seems no obvious evolutionary advantage in sleep as a sleeping animal is defenceless, cannot feed, cannot take care of its offspring, cannot avoid the risks of being eaten by a predator and cannot have sex and so procreate. The very fact that it is costly suggests that it must be a vital process.
—Brian Winston

At times . . . my photisms take on a rather soothing *flou* quality, and then I see – projected, as it were, upon the inside of the eyelid – grey figures

walking between beehives, or small black parrots gradually vanishing among mountain snows, or a mauve remoteness melting beyond moving masts.
—Vladimir Nabokov

As I consider these matters more carefully, I see so plainly that there are no definitive signs by which to distinguish being awake from being asleep. As a result, I am becoming quite dizzy, and this dizziness nearly convinces me that I am asleep.
—René Descartes

A story is told according to which Saint-Pol-Roux, in times gone by, used to have a notice posted on the door of his manor house . . . every evening before he went to sleep, which read: 'The poet is working'. . . . I believe in the future resolution of [the] two states, dream and reality, which are seemingly so contradictory, into a kind of absolute reality, a surreality, if one may so speak. It is in quest of this surreality that I am going, certain not to find it but too unmindful of my death not to calculate to some slight degree the joys of its possession.
—André Breton

I could be bounded in a nutshell and count myself a king of infinite space, were it not that I have bad dreams.
—William Shakespeare

To shake people up, to wake them from their sleep . . . you are committing a crime and . . . it would be a thousand times better to leave them alone, since when they wake, too, you have nothing to offer them.
—E.M. Cioran

. . . one gust in the damp cedar hissing
Will have the mist right off in half a minute.
You will not grasp the meaning, you will be in it.
—Allen Curnow, 'Out of Sleep'

53

In childhood sleeping and waking baffled me,
and a lifetime of experiments has left me little the wiser –
the nightly withdrawal into the mind, the unpredictable process
of losing control, the disappearance and return of the self.
This river follows its own currents, its own laws.

It is claimed that sleep renews energy, eases
the heart and helps keep the mind in order,
digests the day, sorts memories, harvests
thoughts. So say the scientists with binary minds,
theorising the logic of sleep and glossing over its anarchy.
Yet dreams continue to stitch their crazy quilts
of oddments, mental scraps, obscure omens.

Now the pinging of rain on the roof is fading.
Deepening silence surrounds the quiet mantra
of heart and pulse. The room is pitch black
except for needles of light at the curtain's edge.
I need the world to be pure and simple, but eyelids
closed are still a screen for flickers and reflections
of the mind. I am impatient to change, like water
ready to become steam or harden into ice.
But the present is reluctant to vanish. Thoughts are like
the sea's whisper in a shell as the tide recedes.
If only it were possible to shrink awareness
to a nano-point. But how to reduce the assertion
of myself, the friction of surfaces, the pressure of time?
Insomnia! I wriggle like a wild animal trying
to settle into its den but failing to fit.
Finally before dawn, wrapped in the returning
sounds of rain, my self slowly dissolves
into waves of sleep, like an amphibian returning
once more to the sea. In dreams one is freed
from the laws of physics, but not from a body.

I am in an elegant old villa with high ceilings,
faintly familiar, searching in the half-light
for a lost photo of my father. Excited but anxious,

54

I need to keep my housebreaking and quest secret.
I pull a dusty book from the shelves and riffle
the pages. A butterfly floats out, but no picture.
Clumsily I drop the book, and the crash startles
a large bird in the shadows who takes off
in a squall of wings. I collect my scattered wits.
The wall of unknown books looms, leans in,
packed tight, close to toppling. A maze
Of hiding places. I see a solitary envelope
but as I greedily reach for it, it changes to a rat
or weasel with gleaming eyes and teeth. I jerk
back as though my hand has been savaged, and my spasm
triggers an alarm that will not stop ringing.
The room changes size, and I start tumbling
through space, losing myself to gravity.

Waking begins but the nightmare struggles to continue
unfolding, each world determined to assert
its claims. Moving shadows brush the eyes,
a branch scrapes the window. Then a hand makes
its choice and stretches to silence the alarm. Waking
is like an elevator door opening at the top floor
or sticking one's head through the wall into a different
universe, like the famous fake Renaissance woodcut.

The self must boot up for another day,
but before recalling the codes of this world, I take
time to weigh up its singular presence.
All day it will embody me with its edges and particulars.
I plant my feet on the grain of the wooden floor,
ease a twinge of cramp, and grasp the cold
metal door handle in a world of stubborn
substance. The clatter and smell of the coffee machine
and a thousand other givens return as the amphibian
lumbers onto land. The only person said to have
awakened fully was Buddha. As for me, I'm happy
to be a butterfly or bird dreaming it's a man.

The day is impatient to make its habitual demands.
Before I walk out into the street, I check
my hair is neatly combed and shoes laced,
and seek to tidy my tousled mind. Keeping
up appearances ensures that no one is likely
to question my passport to the land of the living,
the country of sane, awake, adult citizens.

The rain has passed. The human apiary is buzzing.
Rush hour. The road is noisy with children,
bodies in school uniform vibrating with energy.
Each head a unique tangle of neurons
that the night has laboured to grow and repair.

9. DEATH

The man walks into nothing.
The boat sails into nothing.
—Shadi Abdel Salam

D'ailleurs, c'est toujours les autres qui meurent. ('Besides, it's always the others who die.')
—Epitaph on the tombstone of Marcel Duchamp, October 1968

Lorne said . . . 'I learnt that what you perceive on visiting an organisation that you had left some time ago is the same as seen in a bucket of water from which you withdraw your immersed hand. There is no hole left to fill, in the smooth flat unperturbed surface. There is little to indicate that you were ever there.'
—Megan Nicol Reed

The closest closeness which one may have in being towards death as a possibility is as far as possible from anything actual. The more unveiledly this possibility gets understood, the more purely does the understanding penetrate into it as the possibility of the impossibility of any existence at all.
—Martin Heidegger

In paradise, objects and beings, assaulted by light from all sides, cast no shadow. Which is to say that they lack reality, like anything that is unbroached by darkness and deserted by death.
—E.M. Cioran

When the quantum coherence in the microtubules is lost, as in cardiac arrest, or death, the Planck scale quantum information in our heads dissipates, leaks out, to the universe as a whole. The quantum information

57

which has comprised our conscious and unconscious minds during life doesn't completely dissipate, but hangs together because of quantum entanglement.
—Stuart Hameroff

In our deepest convictions, reaching into the very depths of our being, we deserve to live forever. We experience our transitoriness and mortality as an act of violence perpetrated against us.
—Czesław Miłosz

Who cares anything today for a finely-finished death? No one. Even the rich, who could after all afford this luxury of dying in full detail, are beginning to be careless and indifferent; the wish to have a death of one's own is growing ever rarer. A while yet, and it will be just as rare as a life of one's own. Heavens, it's all there. One arrives, one finds a life, ready made, one has only to put it on. One wants to leave or one is compelled to: anyway, no effort: *Voilà votre mort, monsieur.*
—Rainer Maria Rilke

The walls of the tattoo parlor where Ty engraved a cortical microcircuit from Ramón y Cajal onto my left arm are graced with an admonition that serves as alternative ending: 'Life's journey is not to arrive at the grave safely, in a well-preserved body, but rather to skid in sideways, totally worn out, shouting, Holy mackerel . . . what a ride!'
—Christof Koch

Though you tumble her in every haystack from here to Paradise, there will be a question at the end and no answer from the night.
—A.R.D. Fairburn, 'Terms of Appointment'

It has come to the notice of the company that employees are dying on their feet and refusing to fall over. This practice must cease forthwith. In future if the foreman notices that an employee has made no movement for two hours, it is his duty to investigate. Any employee found dead on the job,

in an upright position, will be immediately dropped from the payroll.
—Seen on a factory noticeboard

Whoever destroys a soul, it is considered as if he destroyed an entire world.
And whoever saves a life, it is considered as if he saved an entire world.
—*Babylonian Talmud*

The expansion of the universe means that entropy is growing. Everything
is, generally, getting constantly further apart; distances are growing; more
space is appearing without there being more matter. Everything is being
diluted with nothing; more and more degrees of freedom are appearing.
Things are becoming more difficult to describe.
—Tor Nørretranders

Some famous last words: *Kilroy was here.*
Once alive and aware, Kilroy the sloganeer
tried to think outside the square. Now
he's vanished into air and his messages
are smudged and rare. Look on the works
of Kilroy, all ye authors, and despair!
I imagine Kilroy as an old man I saw
in the nursing home, lying on a bed staring
at the ceiling, perhaps worrying about his medical bills
or trying to ride out a stomach ache.
Or was he racking his brains for a final riposte
as the young Rainer Maria Rilke advised:
'One ought to wait and gather sense and sweetness
a whole life long, and a long life
if possible, and then, quite at the end, one might
perhaps be able to write ten lines.'
Was this old man sifting through all the ceilings
he had ever gazed at, desperate for a summation, an epiphany,
a final visionary payoff? If it were me
my eye would be distracted by a fly, by the peeling wallpaper
or the sunset light and shadow on the shabby ceiling.

Death is a oncer which no one can foresee.
We contemplate it from many angles and ponder
many images. In boyhood my war and cowboy
comics gave me that frisson with their danse macabre
of combat at close quarters by square-jawed action
figures, who hurled their ultimate speech balloons
into a storm of bullets, before going for a Burton,
buying a one-way ticket, or biting the dust,
their spasm of blood and guts rendered stylish
by the Ben-Day dots. Adults were more inclined
to moralise but they too turned death into conceit –
met his maker, gave up the ghost, went
the way of all flesh, paid his debt
to Nature – so many ways to come to nothing.

Now funerals and tangi have become more frequent,
even the most distant or dutiful ritual can darken
my day and jolt me with its sense of finality
as verbs are transformed into the past tense.
I'm haunted by a comment of Marcus Aurelius:
'Let thy every action, word and thought
be that of one who is prepared at any moment
to quit this life.' He was in the thick of a war.
At the graveside I feel the weight of the disaster,
hear the Kaddish, try to ignore the rain,
deliver my three spadefuls, leaving the spade
in the clay for the next mourner. Differences lapse;
here there is room only for compassion.

Nothing becomes a palpable presence. Once
it was claimed the earth was flat and the ocean ended
in tremendous waterfalls over which ships plunged
to destruction. Not everyone believed this
but it's true that a precipice awaits all of us in the end.
In new wave style, we may ride a spaceship
into the vortex of a black hole and lose our lifetime's
battle with gravity. On the very brink, time
may dilate, but nothing can prevent the final plunge.

The day after the funeral, horizons have returned
to normal, although I feel guilty to have outlived a friend.
The rain has freshened colours and shaken loose
the smells of vegetation. A dog snuffles through
the bushes, curious to get to the bottom of things. In Arcadia
creatures are insistent, present without leave,
full not of God but simply of themselves.
Our ship with its motley crew is still afloat.

November first is El Dia de los Muertos, the Day
of the Dead, a Mexican holiday with altars and marigolds,
dancing skeletons, sugar and chocolate skulls,
candles and tequila, to celebrate those who are gone
and to give the rest a foretaste of *pan de muerto*.
Even here on the far side of the world
this day casts the shadow of *duende* on this scene
of empty streets, grey clouds, and silence.
I think of objects encountered in distant museums –
Ivan Albright's room dedicated to dust
or the shadow of a man burned into stone steps
or a piano in a Holocaust museum with its lid sealed,
its last chord imagined to be still fading.
I once visited a morgue where the flesh of the naked body
on a slab was like rubber, its total stillness
in eerie contrast with the nimble fingers of the pathologist,
as businesslike as an electrician checking a fusebox.

It's rumoured that Sigmund Freud had an illusion painting
he sometimes tested on patients who could see
a beautiful naked couple having sex,
or else a skull. These images of flesh and bone
struggled to be apart, but they were forced to remain
in permanent superposition, like a quantum cat in a box.

My friends go drinking to celebrate the Day of the Dead,
and imagine apt ways to die in harness.
The poet will chew a pencil and contract lead

poisoning. The scriptwriter will be zapped by his computer.
The architect will foolishly visit the construction site
of his high-rise. The cameraman will be too busy framing
to notice where his feet are headed. The dancer
will take for granted the large spotlight above her head.
The sculptor will fail to resist a final stroke
of the chisel. The academic will reach for a reference book
at the top of packed shelves. An overworked cymbal
will fly to decapitate the drummer. In our swansongs
we dare to compete with heroes of history – Pietro
Aretino who died from too much laughing,
Aeschylus flattened by a tortoise dropped by an eagle
who mistook his head for a rock, or Li Po
who leaned over the side of a boat to kiss
the moon's reflection in the water. Other deaths
are less poetic: Roland Barthes, immersed
in thought, failed to notice a laundry van;
Gabriel Fauré forgot his bike helmet;
Isadora Duncan wore a scarf too long;
astronomer Tycho Brahe died of a burst
bladder, reluctant to interrupt a deep conversation.

My friends have a common preference for their final
destination: a small, well-lit tomb with unlimited
paper, ink, coffee, liquor, books
and music. In such a cabin, you may forever
continue peacefully revising your last words.

In the land of the living, death is a topic on which no one
maintains a constant tone. Laughter can segue
into panic, and out of a clear blue sky
something very heavy may suddenly drop,
like a medical crisis. The hospital cooks me in a scanner
then leaves me to stew in a drab waiting room,
too shook up to read. The globe of my mind
fills with snow. One test result could shatter
my mood and unsettle all my future plans.

But today I'm lucky – a minor problem, which a small
operation can mend, like a new patch of roofing
which will keep out the rain for a few more years.
I leave my specialist poring over his X-rays.
His freeze-frame of the brain is a blue landscape
of cells and neurons, the earth seen from space.
Or is Paik's Buddha contemplating his television screen?

After the scare, my afternoon is a reprieve, a special
gift. I opt to spend it at home with a glass
of wine on the window seat and the hefty science
book I've delayed reading because of the time required.
It covers everything from the Big Bang to black
holes. By next century its universe will probably
seem as quaint and obsolete as a flat earth.
But this afternoon's amnesty allows me to indulge
in the human fantasy of the bucket list – my wish
is to live long enough to understand.

10. EVOLUTION

The universe was brought into being in a less than fully formed state, but was gifted with the capacity to transform itself from unformed matter into a truly marvellous array of structure and life forms.
—Saint Augustine, c. 398 CE

All that has been learned empirically about evolution in general and mental process in particular suggests that the brain is a machine assembled not to understand itself, but to survive.
—E.O. Wilson

Not I, some child, born in a marvellous year,
Will learn the trick of standing upright here.
—Allen Curnow, 'The Skeleton of the Great Moa in the Canterbury Museum, Christchurch'

Though my fingers never evolved for linguistic communication, the moment I began to use them to type words on a keyboard, they came to function for this end. . . . The potential of my fingers to assume this function was simply not excluded by the constraints they acquired due to natural selection.
—Terrence W. Deacon

You first have processing of information, and various automatisms of the kind done by the dorsal stream, and then some stage in evolution created a representation of the representation for other purposes. The question is, what are those other purposes? You could say, isn't it redundant: why create another representation of the representation? The answer is, it isn't. . . . This is what we call thinking. . . . It was a quantum leap in the mind of an ape.
—Vilayanur S. Ramachandran

Why is the human brain the most complex object known to exist in the universe? Because the elaborations of the mammalian brain that promoted the survival of the organism overshot the mark in our case.
—Marilynne Robinson

How do you know but ev'ry Bird that cuts the airy way,
Is an immense world of delight, clos'd by your senses five?
—William Blake, 'A Memorable Fancy'

A new era in evolution. . . . A glow ripples outward from the first spark of conscious reflection. The point of ignition grows larger. The fire spreads in ever widening circles till finally the whole planet is covered with incandescence. . . . It is really a new layer, the 'thinking layer', which . . . has spread over and above the world of plants and animals.
—Pierre Teilhard de Chardin

The term 'evolution' has entered popular consciousness in powerful ways, and the accepted lay definition can be summed up as 'progressive change' . . . something that has evolved is better than something that preceded it. . . . In Darwin's original work, no such judgement is made, and biologists and palaeontologists agree that evolution . . . does not include such a value judgement.
—Mark Erickson

The world and all that is in it is actually a higgledy-piggledy, wasteful mess. Each evolutionary stage necessarily built on one, and only one, stage that went before it and used random genetic mutations as they popped up. If no useful mutation showed up in a newly fraught environmental situation, an evolutionary line simply became extinct: evolutionary history is littered with wasteful, meaningless dead-ends. Perhaps human beings are another.
—David Lewis-Williams

After AI scientists become more capable than human scientists, research in artificial intelligence would be carried out by machines. . . . To such a fast mind, the external world would appear to run in slow motion. . . . We cannot hope to compete with such machine brains. . . . Then our fate will depend on the will of such a 'superintelligence', much as the fate of gorillas today depends more on what we do than on gorillas themselves.

—Nick Bostrom

Evolution today is a range of computer games
from 'Amoebas' to 'Microbe Kombat' to 'Neuro Evolving
Robotic Operatives'. We're warned that 'evogames' contain
'horror, fear, violence and suggestive themes',
but now we're able to 'guide and control evolution'.
They've even made it a party game for iPhones
where players start as amoebas, become cockroaches,
then rabbits and gorillas, before graduating to humans
with suitable actions and sounds for each phase.

We needed a big picture, and evolution fills
the bill, though humans may be only
a detail in the corner. Our genes still carry the tale
of the tribe – back a few billion years
to when a lucky mix of chemicals invented
creatures with sensitive skins and the urge to know
the world and turn the landscape into a field of energy,
a bubbling soup of feeling. Limbs learned
to touch and choose, bodies to fight or unite.
Facts became reflections and the mirror grew.
Surviving was almost a full-time job but consciousness
wanted a chance to ponder its own ambience,
awareness of self igniting like marsh gas.
Thus humans emerged as brains at their hungriest
and turned the history of the world into an inside story.

Yet cautious scientists see no plan
and no planner, so they leave out the ladder
of progress and view all species as equal,
good of their kind, masters of adaptation.

I value their omnibus respect for life
but still feel nostalgia for the spirit of evolution –
a ghost in the machine? – who sings of the growth of thought.
This spirit haunts the status quo and spooks it
with talk of change, progress and positive selection.

Cave painting was never merely a tool
for survival. I'm at my table, not painting
bison with ochre pigments but scrawling words.
I started my morning reading emails and paying
bills – the daily business, necessary protection –
but then chose simply to collect my thoughts.
I pause to watch an ant's straight line
across the table, heading past my cup
towards a tiny residue of breakfast toast.
This ancient hunter and gatherer advances slowly
and I resist the temptation to squash it, but sternly
remove the crumbs, turning its oasis into a mirage.

Out the window is Truman, the sapote tree
(Cochitzapotl), which I have watched grow from a seedling,
a lateral thinker whose limbs grope for space.
Its current resident, the tui, has much to say –
it clicks, cackles, coughs, and richly chimes
sounding its yawp over the roofs of the suburb
while I struggle to write. I have more DNA
and will probably outlive it but I envy its wings.
It sings even when executing fancy aerobatics.
Birds evolved from dinosaurs, but now the tui
is one more species struggling to survive.
I can't make sense of its language or thoughts
but I can at least offer this eater of nectar
a secure tree with fermenting fruit and flowers.

Saturday offers time for writing and distractions
like the tui or watching the cat on the porch
prick up her ears. Hard-wired to hunt

birds, she would once have darted up Truman
but is now too old. Instead she turns
to a plant and licks drops of rain from its leaves,
listens again to her bête noire, then enters
with effort through the cat door. She acknowledges
this man with a meow, pads over, and curls up
nearby on the window seat. She has utterly
no interest in whether she gets written about.
We both like company, but not too much.

Each species focuses on its own priorities
though her closeness is not only a function of food.
We have lived with each other's strangeness
for sixteen years, and now despite the myth
of nine lives, her time is running out.
I remain curious why she's not more curious
about machines, but I guess she knows what she needs
for a streamlined life. Perhaps I cut as many
corners. We're fellow mammals, and while our last
common ancestor was 90 million years
ago we still share the same chromosomes,
X and Y (which is bad genetic karma
as it makes cats ideal for lab experiments).
Her flexible ears know sounds too high
or faint for mine, her sense of smell is sharper,
and her large pupils make her deft in the dark.
Granted, my colour equipment is more evolved,
and I write while she sleeps, but her eyes flicker
since she is dreaming in her own way.
We human animals waste time, are easily
distracted, and our thoughts crawl like ants,
but we can boast of inventing words and sentences,
our patented mirror, however distorting and flawed.

There is an elephant in the room – this computer,
an evolutionary change happening in our lifetime,
reducing our customs to fossils and converting

68

our children to new formats. As the Digital Age
powers on, I look wistfully at my books,
pen and notepad, and see that language is mutating.
Now the Web is a field of seething energies,
ready to extend and pool consciousness, is this
the transformation of the world to a unified virtual mind
or merely another noisy playground and marketplace?

When robots start building smarter robots,
the days of organic intelligence may be numbered.
I try to imagine a mind that views humans
from the height we tend to assume when we think
of animals. What could such a paragon create?
Art in more than four dimensions, music
beyond our few octaves of hearing, mathematics
that perfectly portrays the world, attention so vast
that ours seems a tiny periscope? Or will the outcome
be not evolution but the first complete break
with the story of DNA – artificial intelligence as a metal
and plastic emptiness, a desert of silenced neurons?

11. GODS

Pope Benedict XVI marked the holiest night of the year for Christians by stressing that humanity isn't a random product. . . . 'If man were merely a random product of evolution in some place on the margins of the universe, then his life would make no sense or might even be a chance of nature,' he said. 'But no, reason is there at the beginning: creative, divine nature.'
—*New Zealand Herald*

Is God happy? . . . Certainly we are told that God loves his creatures, and love, at least in the human world, is an emotion. But love is a source of happiness when it is reciprocated, and God's love is reciprocated by only some of His subjects, by no means all: some do not believe that He exists, some do not care whether He exists or not, and others hate Him, accusing Him of indifference in the face of human pain and misery. If He is not indifferent, but subject to emotion like us, He must live in a constant state of sorrow.
—Leszek Kołakowski

No egocentric particulars occur in the language of physics. Physics views space-time impartially, as God might be supposed to view it; there is not, as in perception, a region which is especially warm and intimate and bright, surrounded in all directions by growing darkness.
—Bertrand Russell

The beginning of modern science can be dated from the time when such general questions as, 'How was the universe created? What is matter made of? What is the essence of life?' were replaced by such limited questions as 'How does a stone fall? How does water flow in a tube? How does blood circulate in vessels?' This substitution had an amazing result.
—François Jacob

Shiva's dance – in the words of [Ananda] Coomaraswamy – is 'the clearest image of the activity of God which any art or religion can boast of.' As the god is a personification of Brahman, his activity is that of Brahman's myriad manifestations in the world. The dance of Shiva is the dancing universe; the ceaseless flow of energy going through an infinite variety of patterns that melt into one another.

—Fritjof Capra

. . . it is possible to imagine a supermind existing since the creation, encompassing all the fundamental fields of nature, and taking upon itself the task of converting an incoherent big bang into the complex and orderly cosmos we now observe; all accomplished entirely within the framework of the laws of physics. . . . We could describe this state of affairs by saying that . . . the universe is a mind: a self-observing as well as self-organising system.

—Paul Davies

Our self-proclaimed title of Homo sapiens, the wise or discerning human, is surely a hope rather than a reality. Most of the time we are only Homo credens, the species that needs to believe as much as it needs to breathe.

—Bernard J. Baars

Obviously God was a solution, and obviously none so satisfactory will ever be found again.

—E.M. Cioran

Why in heaven did God decide to create
the world? At thirteen and restless with religious secrets
I was desperate to know. Adult life baffled me
and its scary cost of admission demanded a rationale.
But when I consulted Bible Class comrades
they saw my questions as playing with fire.
I could ask God on Judgement Day
and until then it was an act of human arrogance,

an opening for the Devil to inject his sly doubts.
Too much curiosity killed the catechism.
So, at the edge of the world, I ran smack
into a blank wall. But if God only wanted faith,
why give us so strong an appetite for questions?
If He lived purely on an absolute plane,
then human questions must fall short, but this
was a spirit who chose to dirty His hands with the chaos
of the world – Our Father, peerless but personal
enough for me to keep asking Him 'Why?'

On a lonely day I began to wonder if isolation
had got Him down, stewing unique and singular
in His own sanctity. Did He invent disciples
as a mirror to represent and contemplate His existence?

At school we were conducting science experiments,
which often bombed. Suppose we were also guinea
pigs, another of God's many tryouts?
Had He tired of the ideal, the abstract, the infinite,
and grown curious to explore otherness, greed,
ugliness, all things ordinary – His opposites,
for which we provided a copious case history?

My Bible Class colleagues were aghast at these ideas.
God as a Trinity could not be lonely. If creation
needed a reason, it was the overflow of His love.
Our minister was also adamant that the only motive
for creating the world was kindness – to bless believers
with the joys of nature, fellowship, and family. If
there were storms and shadows, God was heightening
light and colour by a subtle use of contrast.

I shared this painterly vision of a perfect artist
for another year, but grew troubled by its disregard
for collateral damage. I came to imagine His cool
viewing of human history as like a soap opera,

a reality show rich in black humour.
It takes a village to build a church, to raise
a child to fear and believe, a tiny village
preaching one big idea, an idea
that alone I saw shrivel like a star, slowly
collapsing to a cold remnant, a white dwarf.
But what if I was wrong? Afraid at night,
I whispered my old prayer: if I should die
before I wake. Now the flock eyed me
as an outsider, fallen publicly from grace like an arrogant
actor forgetting his part, incensing the audience.

Please leave me alone to work this out
in my own head! And in that space God shrank
gradually to human proportions, just another
parent or teacher – His power to harm me faded,
His world melted like a mirage. For the first time
I'd stepped outside the life in which I was born.

In my last dream of God, He went out with a bang.
The effort of creation had proved so intense
He had shattered in the process. Now we lived in the midst
of the fragments and a tiny piece of Him was lodged
in each of our heads. If we sought a rationale
for the world, nobody was left to ask but ourselves.

What ground is left? This landscape where generations glimpsed
God, immersed in His timeless presence, is now
a demolition site, a wide open space.
The light is sharp, the scene bristles with ordinariness.
Half a century and many arguments older,
I have become an adult, a parent, even a teacher.
The question changed from why to create a world
to a different mystery – how to construct a life.
Now time is running out. Have I kept the faith?
I've been through religions, a reluctant heretic – let
a hundred gods and goddesses bloom! – but each
answer finally gave up the ghost, shrinking

to the scale of an old book, one of many.
Over the years I've been pleased to visit churches
when there's something to celebrate or mourn; but I scoff
when the worldly who ditched their choirboy values
develop last-minute fears of the Great Examiner.
Funerals have the magic to transform rogues into saints.
Yet when time comes to sail over the edge
even the worst can be excused a blindfold or prayer.

The church shines its spotlight on earthly things
as props in God's theatre, but daylight reduces
the stage to a tawdry set. The ultimate Auteur
vanishes from sight, though popes and patriarchs, gurus
and ayatollahs still shout stage directions.
But we are all born with a hunger for meaning, for a tall
view from which the world gains depth, pattern
and purpose. The kind of space religion invented
can still be precious when kept off-limits to Mammon
and Moloch, swept clear of dogmas and taboos,
'no god' as a credo without a Vatican,
'capable,' as Keats put it, 'of being in doubts.'

I end as I began, with a human figure walking,
moving in its cloud of limitations, fragile and transient
but nosy and alert. The old books are silent.
The season is winter, the sky an unpredictable mix
Of light and dark with clouds tussling for dominance.
Bare tree branches tremble in the wind.
To my eyes these objects carry no hint
Of a maker's brand, but human life gives
Them depth, curious gifts from the marrow of the world.

No closing hymn or *deus ex machina* –
only an occasional song from my friendly ghost.
The darkened sky resolves its suspense by rain.
A jutting roof offers partial shelter.
Beside me there are new graffiti on the garage door

Which some kid has sprayed in wildstyle tags
I can't decipher. They make me nostalgic for Old
School symbols such as Kilroy, his nose over
a wall at the very end of the world. I pass
the time by imagining my open-ended epitaph:

*Kilroy was (briefly) here. The reasons how
and why are partly clear. There's rain in the air
and he's much the worse for wear, but still
a citizen of the biosphere, not eager to disappear.*

*Happy to wait round for the next idea,
he no longer pins his hopes on prayer.
His faith is simply (simply?) to be aware.*

AUTHOR'S NOTE

What I have written may be described as 'a philosophical poem', but, if so, the emphasis needs to fall on the word 'poem' since an academic philosopher would have approached the subject very differently.

Too much of today's poetry seems to me narrowly focused on the self. Language poetry has opened things up by shifting the emphasis from self to language, but on this occasion I have been drawn to something different – an expanded sense of self I call 'consciousness'.

Contemporary writers and artists have tended to avoid getting 'too serious' since the postmodern mood of irony descended over the arts. Cynicism is a totally understandable response to today's social world, but in terms of tone this has created too large a no-go area. As Lewis Hyde once observed in an essay on John Berryman, 'Irony has only emergency use. Carried over time it is the voice of the trapped who have come to enjoy their cage.'

Of course, seriousness comes in many forms, and focusing on the strangeness of the mind – 'where it feels like what it feels like' – runs the risk of sounding earnest and adolescent. I was certainly obsessed with problems of meaning as a teenager, but life has never stopped raising similar questions, and it has not become easier to find answers. Now I am also a lot older, and sadly aware of having outlived some talented friends (Leigh Davis and Julian Dashper, to mention just two). My response here is to go back to basics. Not that being serious has to mean being solemn, for European and Latin American writers (among others) have shown that poetry can be philosophical or conceptual without being clunky or academic.

The book is organised thematically. Each section is a freewheeling meditation on a theme. The themes are as basic and serious as they come, but they are issues that everybody will sometimes encounter and argue about. Since the overall theme is 'consciousness', the second section forms the heart of the work. The other sections may be seen as radiating out from this centre. The poem is open-ended. What it currently contains are the concerns of a particular year, many of its ideas and memories having emerged in the course of my walks during that time.

Each section begins with a set of quotations. I like the way in which each quotation approaches a common theme from its own perspective and with its own feeling for language. By implication, each idea challenges all the ideas round it. The authors tend to be scientists, poets, philosophers or journalists. I see pure science as an important source, powered by recent discoveries in areas such as neuroscience and astronomy. Scientists are uninhibited about being serious, and some are as idiosyncratic and evocative as poets. A number of ancient scientists (or 'natural philosophers') presented their work in poetic form. I like the motto that Mahmoud Darwich took from the 10th-century Arab writer Abû Hayyân Al-Tawhîdî: 'The most beautiful speech is that which situates itself between poetry that looks like prose and prose that looks like poetry.'

While a tight structure would not have suited the project, I wanted form because of the energy it creates. I am tired of the loose free verse found in so much contemporary poetry, semi-colloquial speech that reverts to iambic when it wants to pump up the lyricism. Instead I have followed two rules: using a line with five main stresses, and keeping the rhythm changing in order to avoid the cliché of iambic or any other smooth metrical pattern. One section of the poem (the second) has a different mode of organisation.

In my treatment of themes such as death and religion, I have no wish to imply disrespect towards individuals who have different beliefs or customs. I endorse freedom of thought and value the seriousness of my religious (as well as my secular) friends, and am grateful for opportunities to debate with them.

I want to acknowledge my family. Its members are all very important to me, even though they make few appearances in this poem, through which various speakers (sometimes, but not always, myself) ride as introspective and restless lone rangers. The work is dedicated to my wife Shirley, whose support is the main reason my life has been balanced and positive enough to undertake this unsettled, questioning project.

—Roger Horrocks

REFERENCES

1. Walking

—'He who sees': Aristotle, quoted in Giorgio Agamben, *What Is an Apparatus? and Other Essays*, trans. David Kishnik and Stefan Predatella (Stanford, CA: Stanford University Press, 2009), 32.

—'Never did I exist so completely': Jean-Jacques Rousseau, *The Confessions of J.J. Rousseau*, Book IV (London: Aldus Society, 1903; Project Gutenberg, 2006).

—'From the sublime to the ridiculous': Attributed to Napoleon Bonaparte, as recorded by Abbé du Pradt, quoted in Archibald Alison, *History of Europe from the Commencement of the French Revolution in 1789, to the Restoration of the Bourbons in 1815*, Vol. 3 (New York: Harper and Brothers, 1844), 593.

—'I am alarmed when it happens': Henry David Thoreau, 'Walking', *Nature / Walking* (Boston, MA: Beacon Press, 1991), 78–79.

—'The primary motor cortex': John J. Ratey, *A User's Guide to the Brain* (New York: Vintage, 2002), 362.

—'According to Lakoff and Johnson': Bernard J. Baars, *In the Theatre of Consciousness: The Workspace of the Mind* (New York: Oxford University Press, 1997), 83.

—'Walk past these houses': Kendrick Smithyman, 'Walk Past These Houses on a Sunday Morning', *An Anthology of New Zealand Verse*, ed. Robert Chapman and Jonathan Bennett (London: Oxford University Press, 1956), 197–98.

—'Solvitur ambulando': Lewis Carroll, 'What the Tortoise Said to Achilles', *Mind* (Vol. 4, No. 14, 1895): 278.

2. Consciousness

—'Annihilating all that's made': Andrew Marvell, 'The Garden', in *Poetry: A Critical and Historical Introduction*, ed. Irving Ribner and Harry Morris (Chicago: Scott Foresman and Company, 1962), 138.

—'Now you have gathered yourself together into yourself': Rainer Maria Rilke, *The Notebooks of Malte Laurids Brigge*, trans. M.D. Herter Norton (New York: W.W. Norton, 1964), 69.

—'Consciousness is a fascinating but elusive phenomenon': N.S. Sutherland, *The International Dictionary of Psychology* (New York: Continuum, 1989), 95.

—'Studying consciousness was simply not the thing to do': Antonio Damasio, *The Feeling of What Happens* (San Diego, CA: Harcourt, 1999), 7.

—'I shall often speak': Gilbert Ryle, *The Concept of Mind* (London: Hutchinson, 1949), 15–16.

—'Consciousness, then, is a great delusion': Susan Blackmore, *Consciousness* (New York: Sterling, 2005), 165.

—'It is an interesting exercise': Julian Jaynes, *The Origin of Consciousness in the Breakdown of the Bicameral Mind* (New York: Mariner Books, 2000), 13.

—'Scientific psychology began in the nineteenth century': Michael C. Corballs, *Pieces of Mind: 21 Short Walks around the Human Brain* (Auckland: Auckland University Press, 2011), 2.

—'It is not possible to make consciousness visible': Raymond Tallis, *The Explicit Animal: A Defence of Human Consciousness* (Houndmills: Macmillan, 1991), 222.

—'Consciousness is not something that happens inside us': Alva Noë, *Out of Our Heads* (New York: Hill and Wang, 2009), xii.

—'I still remember': Giulio Tononi, *Phi: A Voyage from the Brain to the Soul* (New York: Pantheon Books, 2012), 302–3.

—'Another area of biology': Michael Brooks, 'What We'll Never Know', *New Scientist*, 7 May 2011, 38.

3. Body

—'What, indeed, does man know of himself': Friedrich Nietzsche, *On Truth and Lie in an Extra-moral Sense* (1873), in *The Portable Nietzsche*, trans. Walter Kaufman (New York: Penguin, 1977), 44.

—'I have been living for some time': Charles Olson, 'Human Universe', *Human Universe and Other Essays* (New York: Grove Press, 1967), 6–7.

—'Acute consciousness of having a body': E.M. Cioran, *The Trouble with Being Born*, trans. Richard Howard (New York: Arcade, 1998), 190.

—'By and by, your attention becomes so intensely focused': Jon Krakauer, *Eiger Dreams: Ventures among Men and Mountains* (Guilford, CT: Lyons Press, 1990), 178.

—'Certainly music traverses our bodies': Gilles Deleuze, *Francis Bacon: The Logic of Sensation*, trans. Daniel W. Smith (Minneapolis, MN: University of Minnesota Press, 2004), 46–47.

—'Tiny machines called ribosomes': Christopher Potter, *You Are Here* (London: Hutchinson, 2009), 222.

—'Apart from feeling that my inside is a big black hole': Len Lye, 'Black Jar', *Body English: Text and Images by Len Lye*, ed. Roger Horrocks (Auckland: Holloway Press, 2009).

—'Science tells us that we are merely beasts': Vilayanur S. Ramachandran, *The Tell-Tale Brain: A Neuroscientist's Quest for What Makes Us Human* (New York: Norton, 2011), 291.

—'I envisage our brains': Miguel A.L. Nicolelis, 'Mind Out of Body', *Scientific American*, February 2011, 63.

4. Language

—'Languages are something of a mess': Joshua Foer, 'Utopian for Beginners', *New Yorker*, 24 and 31 December 2012, 86.

—'What a sentence means': Terence W. Deacon, *Incomplete Nature: How Mind Emerged from Matter* (New York: W.W. Norton, 2012), 1–2.

—'The kind of poem I produced in those days': Vladimir Nabokov, *Speak, Memory: An Autobiography Revisited* (New York: Alfred A. Knopf (Everyman's Library), 1999), 169.

—'For a man's problem': Charles Olson, 'Projective Verse', in *Selected Writings*, ed. Robert Creeley (New York: New Directions), 25.

—'Look hard at nature': Allen Curnow, 'There Is a Pleasure in the Pathless Woods', *Trees Effigies Moving Objects* (Wellington: Catspaw Press, 1972), poem 16.

—'Flowers, dew, stars, skies': Janet Frame, *An Autobiography* (Auckland: Century Hutchinson, 1989), 123–24.

—'Animals in the wild': Michael C. Corballis, *From Hand to Mouth: The Origins of Language* (Princeton, NJ: Princeton University Press, 2002), 37.

—'I fully agree with Schopenhauer': Jacques Hadamard, *An Essay on the Psychology of Invention in the Mathematical Field* (Princeton, NJ: Princeton University Press, 1945).

—'Niels Bohr, in conversation': Nick Laird, 'Quantum Poetics', *The Guardian*, 19 July 2008.

—'Music is arguably the most direct': Robin Maconie, *The Concept of Music* (Oxford: Clarendon Press, 1993), 67.

5. Melancholia

—'I went to the radio interview', Neil Young, 'On the Beach', *On the Beach*, Reprise, 1974.

—'I had my first conscious feeling of an outside sadness': Janet Frame, *An Autobiography* (Auckland: Century Hutchinson, 1989), 12–13.

—'In young people': Friedrich Nietzsche, quoted in H.A. Reyburn et al., *Nietzsche: The Story of a Human Philosopher* (London: Macmillan, 1948), 66–67.

—'The feeling that life is essentially inadequate': William Empson, *Versions of Pastoral*, 3rd edn (London: Chatto and Windus), 1968, 114–15.

—'first and last things': Vladimir Nabokov, *Speak, Memory: An Autobiography Revisited* (New York: Alfred A Knopf (Everyman's Library), 1999), 9.

—'[Nabokov] has remarked': Brian Boyd, *Vladimir Nabokov: The American Years* (Princeton, NJ: Princeton University Press, 1993), 561.

—'Genuine boredom has not yet arrived': Martin Heidegger, 'What is Metaphysics?' (1929), trans. Thomas Sheehan, in 'Reading Heidegger's "What is Metaphysics?"' in *The New Yearbook for Phenomenology and Phenomenological Studies I* (2001), Google eBook, 110.

—'he just wants to lie in the sand': Wisława Szymborska, 'A Film from the Sixties', *Poems New and Collected 1957–1997* (Orlando, FL: Harcourt, 2000), 94.

6. Self

—'Life first arose': Christopher Potter, *You Are Here: A Portable History of the Universe* (New York: Harper Perennial, 2010), 105.

—'What is the work of works for man': Pierre Teilhard de Chardin, *The Phenomenon of Man* (New York: Harper Perennial, 2008), 261.

—'[The atom] enters the bloodstream': Primo Levi, *The Periodic Table*, quoted in Martin Rees in *Before the Beginning: Our Universe and Others* (London: Simon and Schuster, 1997), 19.

—'As a rule, New Zealanders': Carl Elliott, 'Mind Game', *New Yorker*, 6 September 2010, 42.

—'I no more wrote': Delmore Schwartz, 'I am a Book I neither Wrote nor Read', *Selected Poems 1938–1958* (New York, New Directions, 1967), 200.

—'Suddenly I was alone': E.M. Cioran, *The Trouble with Being Born*, trans. Richard Howard (New York: Arcade, 1998), 211.

—'The Western conception of the person': Clifford Geertz, *Local Knowledge: Further Essays in Interpretive Anthropology*, (New York: Basic Books, 1983), 59.

—'I'm really just a little window': Daniel Wegner in Susan J. Blackmore, *Conversations on Consciousness* (Oxford: Oxford University Press), 255.

—'The PSM [phenomenal self-model] of Homo sapiens': Thomas Metzinger, *The Ego Tunnel* (New York: Basic Books, 2009), 4–5.

—'Man at his peril': Charles Olson, 'Human Universe', *Human Universe and Other Essays* (New York: Grove Press, 1967), 11.

—'It camps in the Rocky Mountains': Adam Zagajewski, 'The Self', *Selected Poems*, trans. Renata Gorczynski (London: Faber and Faber, 2004), 31.

—'Mind and behaviour are the moment-to-moment results': Antonio Damasio, *Self Comes to Mind: Constructing the Conscious Brain* (New York: Pantheon, 2010), 312.

—'To study the self': Dogen, quoted in Hee-jin Kim, *Eihei Dogen, Mystical Realist* (Somerville, MA: Wisdom Publications, 2004), 125.

—'Tell me, why is it hard': Neil Young, 'Tell Me Why', *After the Gold Rush*, Reprise, 1970.

7. Micro/Macro

—'The universe may', Piet Hein, quoted in Martin Rees, *Just Six Numbers* (New York: Basic Books, 2000), 102.

—'This ultimate stock we have devised to name', Lucretius, *On the Nature of Things [De Rerum Natura]*, c. 59 BCE, trans. William Ellery Leonard (Mineola, NY: Dover, 2004), 3.

—'And he showed me more': Julian of Norwich, c. 1400, quoted in Edward Harrison, *Masks of the Universe: Changing Ideas on the Nature of the Universe* (Cambridge: Cambridge University Press, 2003), 276.

—'The fluctuations from which clusters': Martin Rees, *Before the Beginning: Our Universe and Others* (London: Simon and Schuster, 1997), 182.

—'A well-known feature of quantum fields': Brian Greene, *The Hidden Reality: Parallel Universes and the Deep Laws of the Cosmos* (New York: Vintage, 2011), 284.

—'The universe seems to be a machine': Christopher Potter, *You Are Here: A Portable History of the Universe* (New York: Harper Perennial, 2010), 137.

—'There are lots of concepts': John R. Searle, *Mind: A Brief Introduction* (New York: Oxford University Press, 2004), 120.

—'The mind . . . works on the data it receives': William James, 1890, quoted in Tor Nørretranders, *The User Illusion: Cutting Consciousness Down to Size* (New York: Penguin, 1999), 177.

—'To get a sense of them': E.M. Cioran, *The Temptation to Exist*, trans. Richard Howard (Chicago, IL: University of Chicago Press, 1998), 153–54.

8. Sleeping and Waking

—'Life is really more fun': Tor Nørretranders, *The User Illusion: Cutting Consciousness Down to Size* (New York: Penguin, 1999), 416.

—'Every human being is fully an artist': Friedrich Nietzsche, *The Birth of Tragedy*, ed. Raymond Geuss and Ronald Speirs (Cambridge: Cambridge University Press, 1999), 15–16.

—'The simple self': Antonio Damasio, *Self Comes to Mind: Constructing the Conscious Brain* (New York: Pantheon, 2010), 186.

—'in dreams we are not only': J. Allan Hobson, in *The Blackwell Companion to Consciousness*, ed. Max Velmans and Susan Schneider (Malden, MA: Blackwell, 2009), 108.

—'All species that have been studied': Brian Winston, *The Human Mind and How to Make the Most of It* (London: Bantam, 2004), 151.

—'At times . . . my photisms': Vladimir Nabokov, *Speak, Memory: An Autobiography Revisited* (New York: Vintage, 1989), 34.

—'As I consider these matters': René Descartes, 'Meditations on First Philosophy', in *Classics of Western Philosophy* (6th ed), ed. Steven M. Cahn (Indianapolis, IN: Hackett, 2002), 61.

—'A story is told': André Breton, 'Manifesto of Surrealism (1924)', in *Poems for the Millennium*, Vol. 1, ed. Jerome Rothenberg and Pierre Joris (Berkeley,

CA: University of California Press, 1995), 469.

—'I could be bounded in a nutshell': William Shakespeare, *The Tragedy of Hamlet, Prince of Denmark*, Act 2 Scene 2, ed. Barbara A. Mowat and Paul Werstine (New York: Simon and Schuster, 2012), 99.

—'To shake people up': E.M. Cioran, *The Trouble with Being Born*, trans. Richard Howard (New York: Arcade, 1998), 202.

—'one gust in the damp cedar hissing': Allen Curnow, 'Out of Sleep', *Early Days Yet: New and Collected Poems 1941–1997* (Auckland: Auckland University Press), 218.

9. Death

—'The man walks into nothing': *The Night of Counting the Years* [film], directed by Shadi Abdel Salam (Egypt: Merchant Ivory Productions, 1969).

—'Lorne said': Megan Nicol Reed, 'In Memoriam', *Sunday Star-Times*, 18 September 2011.

—'The closest closeness': Martin Heidegger, *Being and Time*, trans. John Macquarrie and Edward Robinson (San Francisco, CA: Harper SanFrancisco, 1962), 306.

—'In paradise, objects and beings': E.M. Cioran, *The Trouble with Being Born*, trans. Richard Howard (New York: Arcade, 1998), 195.

—'When the quantum coherence': Stuart Hameroff, in *Conversations on Consciousness*, ed. Susan Blackmore (New York: Oxford University Press, 2007), 124.

—'In our deepest convictions': Czesław Miłosz, *Miłosz's ABCs*, trans. Madeline G. Levine (New York: Farrar, Straus and Giroux, 2002), 9.

—'Who cares anything today': Rainer Maria Rilke, *The Notebooks of Malte Laurids Brigge*, trans. M.D. Herter Norton (New York: W.W. Norton, 1964), 17.

—'The walls of the tattoo parlour': Christof Koch, *Consciousness: Confessions of a Romantic Reductionist* (Cambridge, MA: MIT Press, 2012), 171.

—'Though you tumble': A.R.D. Fairburn, 'Terms of Appointment', *The Penguin Book of New Zealand Verse*, ed. Allen Curnow (Harmondsworth, Middlesex: Penguin, 1960), 157.

—'Whoever destroys a soul': Mishnah Sanhedrin 4:5, *Babylonian Talmud*, Tractate Sanhedrin 37a.

— 'the expansion of the universe': Tor Nørretranders, *The User Illusion: Cutting Consciousness Down to Size* (New York: Penguin, 1999), 344.

—'One ought to wait and gather sense and sweetness': Rilke, *The Notebooks of Malte Laurids Brigge*, 26.

10. Evolution

—'The universe was brought into being': St Augustine, paraphrased by Howard J. Van Till and quoted in Martin Rees, *Just Six Numbers: The Deep Forces That Shape the Universe* (New York: Basic Books, 2000), 103.

—'All that has been learned empirically': E.O. Wilson, *Consilience: The Unity of Knowledge* (New York: Knopf, 1998), 96.

—'Not I, some child': Allen Curnow, 'The Skeleton of the Great Moa in the Canterbury Museum, Christchurch', *Collected Poems 1933–1973* (Wellington: A H & A W Reed, 1974), 142.

—'Though my fingers never evolved': Terrence W. Deacon, *Incomplete Nature: How Mind Emerged from Matter* (New York: W.W. Norton, 2012), 542.

—'You first have processing of information': Vilayanur S. Ramachandran in Susan Blackmore, *Conversations on Consciousness* (Oxford: Oxford University Press, 2007), 188.

—'Why is the human brain': Marilynne Robinson, *Absence of Mind* (New Haven, CT: Yale University Press, 2010), 72.

—'How do you know but ev'ry Bird': William Blake, 'A Memorable Fancy', *The Marriage of Heaven and Hell*, *The Complete Poetry and Prose of William Blake* (New York: Anchor Books, 1988), 35.

—'A new era in evolution': Pierre Teilhard de Chardin, *The Phenomenon of Man* (New York: Harper Perennial, 2008), 182.

—'The term "evolution"': Mark Erickson, *Science, Culture and Society: Understanding Science in the 21st Century* (Cambridge, MA: Polity, 2005), 157.

—'The world and all that is in it': David Lewis-Williams, *Conceiving God: The Cognitive Origin and Evolution of Religion* (London: Thames & Hudson, 2010), 127.

—'After AI scientists become more capable': Nick Bostrom, 'Get Ready for the Dawn of Superintelligence', *New Scientist*, 5 July 2014, 26–27.

11. Gods

—'Pope Benedict XVI': *New Zealand Herald*, 25 April 2011, A19.

—'Is God happy?': Leszek Kołakowski, 'Is God Happy?', *The New York Review of Books* (Vol. LIX, No. 20, 20 December 2012): 16.

—'No egocentric particulars': Bertrand Russell, *An Inquiry into Meaning and Truth: The William James Lectures for 1940* (London: Routledge, 1995), 108.

—'The beginning of modern science': François Jacob, 'Evolution and Tinkering', *Science* (Vol. 196, No. 4295, 10 June 1977): 1161–62.

—'Shiva's dance': Fritjof Capra, *The Tao of Physics*, 3rd ed (London: Flamingo, 1992), 271.

—'it is possible to imagine': Paul Davies, *God and the New Physics* (London: Penguin Books, 1990), 210–11.

—'Our self-proclaimed title': Bernard J. Baars, *In the Theatre of Consciousness: The Workspace of the Mind* (New York: Oxford University Press, 1997), 97.

—'Obviously God was a solution': E.M. Cioran, *The Trouble with Being Born*, trans. Richard Howard (New York: Arcade, 1998), 113.

Author's note

—'As Lewis Hyde once observed': Lewis Hyde, 'Alcohol and Poetry: John Berryman and the Booze Talking', *American Poetry Review*, reprinted in *The Pushcart Prize: Best of the Small Presses*, ed. Bill Henderson (New York: Yonkers, 1976).

—'The most beautiful speech is that which situates itself between poetry that looks like prose and prose that looks like poetry': This is my translation of the motto of Mahmoud Darwich's *Comme des Fleurs d'Amandier ou Plus Loin* (Paris: Actes Sud, 2007): 'La plus belle parole est celle qui se situe entre une poésie qui ressemble à la prose et une prose qui ressemble à la poésie.' I regret not knowing the original Arabic version.